roto
works

First published in the United States of America
in 2006 by
Rizzoli International Publications, Inc.
300 Park Avenue South
New York, NY 10010
www.rizzoliusa.com

ISBN-10: 0-8478-2813-1
ISBN-13: 9-780847-828135
LCCN: 2005935563

Front cover : Stillpoints, SCI-ARC
Photographer : James Bassett, Roto Architects, Inc.

Designed by Made in Space, Inc. Los Angeles

Printed and bound in China

2006 2007 2008 2009 2010/ 10 9 8 7 6 5 4 3 2 1

s t i l l p o i n t s

roto<u></u>
works

Michael Rotondi

Clark P. Stevens

Why is the table so long?

I sat down at the table we had just finished building in our office, at Roto. It was the first one completed; sixteen feet long and three feet wide. The top was covered with a sheet of Strathmore paper—a segment of a fifty-foot long roll spooled at one end and rolled up after being used at the other. The table functioned as a surface on which to draw. Whoever was sitting there to talk about a project would be able to draw and talk while others watched or drew as well. This was a table for us to sit around and think visually. The hidden purpose of the table was to periodically re-center the authority with respect to expressed ideas. Nothing was sacred on the table. Once a sketch was made, it belonged to everyone. Nothing was "original" or "proprietary" when sitting and working there. We could draw on top of any other drawing without fear of reprisal. We were sitting there to collectively grow ideas; it was our creative garden. It was conceptually modeled after a barn raising. We were working together for the benefit of all. The specific task was our focal point and the format of our relationship. The real task was to foster cooperation as a counterpoint to competition. We wanted to learn from each other and to develop affinities for each other's differences.

We all understood the concept, but we found it difficult to overcome the years of conditioning. We were taught that ideas and drawings were intellectual property. In our formative years, we were conditioned to believe that we must be original, leaving our unique mark in the world, one that would distinguish us from everyone else. We found this unacceptable.

We believed that it was possible to retain our individual freedoms and the integrity of our ideas as they were incorporated into a greater idea.

This proposition of working together was grounded in certain prior experiences that bore witness to unique benefits. This was not necessarily a better way; merely an alternative. The role of a more experienced member of a team is, first, to create an atmosphere and conditions for others t o express themselves without reservation. Second, to admit that there are other ideas equal to, and perhaps better than, your own. Finally, to listen and learn and then to synthesize all that you can into a bigger idea and give it back to everyone at the table to build upon. The table has had an impact on our methodology and process, but most importantly, on our relationships.

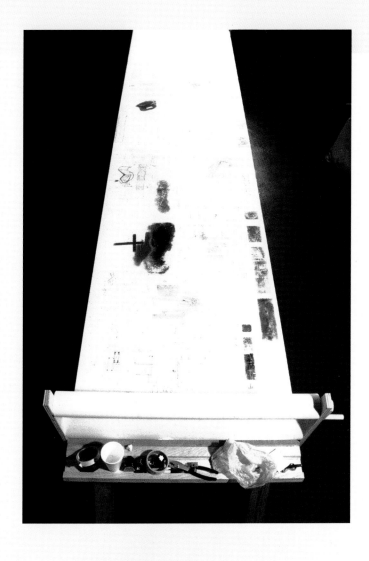

Rotondi is not premature...

...I remember a couple of Bienalles back, walking with Mike Rotondi to look at a huge chunk of ex-World Trade Center steel, now burnt, bent and rusted, on display in front of the American pavilion in Venice, a Barnum and Bailey event accompanied by a number of drawn prognoses, forecasting the future of the site at the end of Manhattan...the exhibition had [nominally] to do with the events of 9.11...but it seemed to Mike to reflect an a priori obligation [perhaps premature] to comment, to explain, and to understand...and to act...

Sounds like Mike...

...I'm not prepared to announce the historic consequences of the fall of the W.T.C...but I recall another discourse on history in which Henry Kissinger allegedly asked Chou en Lai what he thought of the French Revolution, and Chou is supposed to have answered, "I don't know...not enough time has passed yet..."

Rotondi's criteria...

...the [presumed] inevitability of America öber alles—"history is over" [and America's the victor]"—is wobbling...and the whole Trade Center event requires a period of introversion, reflection, patience, even quiet in order to re-imagine the contemporary American experience again in the language of building...

Rotondi's [a] secret...

..."we must go alone," Emerson once said...he and Chou were right...

Split personality [at] work...

...architecture without an a priori pro forma is speculative...Rotondi is the consummate architectural speculator, and his speculations require the insertion of the Rotondi persona into each project... Mike qua Mike is a component of every project program, [in a sense, it's all one project, and all one program], and his architecture takes the consequences...so the work often becomes an investigation of the tensions between possibilities: external requirements contest private explorations...the extrovert versus the introvert...the results are often ragged...necessarily unfinished...and there's no end to the irresolution...it's split personality work...and the means are themselves the ends...

Wait lifting...

...there is, as yet, no form language to communicate that 9.11 "trauma to the ethos," unprecedented on American soil...and this is one reason why the insistence on re-making the New York site has also wandered, unsure of its purpose, obligated by a need to exhibit a re-flexing of the muscles, so the world would know the muscles remain operational...but Rotondi can only lift waits...

Building the unbuildable...

...that American capacity to flex tumbled on 9.11...and for architects and others who follow and record the adventures of architecture in the world today, the collapsed, twin sarcophagi also brought down much of the form language that partnered with the existential musings of Sartre, Genet, Camus, Ionesco, and Demain: pieces but no wholes; the falcon/falconer disconnect, and so on—had become the exegesis for a critically acclaimed spatial [and rhetorical] language of fragility, indeterminacy—the unpredictable twists and turns...but Rotondi never works well with partners...

The end of oil rigs in the North Sea...

...and then, there it was—demolished buildings; demolished rationale at the end of Manhattan...beat that!

...there's another, frequently argued design polemic that was emasculated at the W.T.C...9.11 said goodbye to advocates of technique and progress, manifest in the language of the assembly line and oil rigs in the North Sea...the positivist's science and the tools of technology as both the [erstwhile] prognosis of our future, and the literal language of that future: steel, the means; steel, the end...and then, there was all that steel, that bent positivism, that dismantled prowess, that abused technique [buildings and planes] at the end of Manhattan...

"Through a glass darkly..."

... there we were, staring at that bent chunk that seemed to signify the end of the positivist/techno advocacy, and the hide-and-seek aesthetic...those once poetic idealizations are now visible through the fractured aperture of 9.11...so?

Mike builds Mike...

3

8
+

"How does an acorn become an oak?" we were asked.

This was the first time a question triggered our curiosity and visual imagination simultaneously. *Systemic thinking—seeing the whole, transformation—everything changed in that moment.* The answer was ultimately unknowable yet this was strangely reassuring. We understood that searching for the answer would sustain our curiosity for a lifetime. Curiosity is the mental equivalence of inhaling and exhaling. The question was intended to make us ponder the nature of creation itself.

"We can describe what we see, but we cannot really explain it," the speaker added. We were puzzled by this statement. What was the difference? To us, these words were interchangeable, yet in fact they weren't. Our intellects were being both expanded and fine-tuned. It was a great feeling. Things changed from that point forward. We began to think and talk a lot about PROCESS *(impermanence)*, ORDER *(inter-relationships)* and UNITY *(inter-dependence)*.

For the tree to emerge and exist, its internal code has to continually negotiate external forces and be responsive, yet flexible, within the limits of its genetic code.

Structure and Freedom   In its early phases of growth it changed more radically than it would when it reached a more mature, inevitable state.

Transformation   In subsequent phases of growth it would reveal one of the wonderful truths of certain forms of organic life—as it changed size, its surface area would keep pace with its volume. There was a relativity of growth and a constant similarity of form. This recalls the logarithmic spiral of the nautilus shell: the golden ratio, the system of proportioning that is one of the central ordering systems of modernism, and the basis of the aesthetic system of our teachers.

Embedded within creation (and the creative process) is an implicit ordering system to guide the spontaneous growth of an organism. It does this by setting internal limits (not boundaries) that inform each exchange that takes place internally, with the interface and with the environment in which it was embedded. We had been taught that every action has an equal and opposite reaction.

Reciprocity   The overall system of choices essential to an organism's survival are part of its imprint. The more diverse the system of parts and the more coordinated its response, the greater the duration of life. To ensure survival, it must "remember" all of its prior responses as a frame of reference for current and future decisions.

Memory and action need to be in balance.
Memory is slow.
                    Action is fast.

Conservation and Change   All of this conjured (concurrently verbally and visually), the idea of a system of infinite relationships between all things. Worlds within worlds; all with inextricable complexities and with the simultaneous presence of disparate elements that converge to determine every moment. We imagined that the promise of architecture was to weave it together into a manifold and multifaceted vision of the world.

Unity and Diversity   We repeated out loud, "We can describe it but we cannot explain it." From the moment of conception to the moment of birth, we are the embodiment of creation. For the full term we are in a state of perfect symbiosis. There is a preconscious unity with the environment, an embryonic somatic memory of wholeness and unconditional unity are being imprinted. Two as one. The womb is weightless. It is our "third skin."
At the moment of birth, we experience a profound separation, the most fundamental discontinuity of our lives and one that we spend a lifetime trying to overcome. Our creative work can be a way to reintegrate an apparently complex and discontinuous world, giving us a renewed sense of belonging, a part of a greater whole once again. The birth process can also be one of liberation.

The human body's relationship to the universe may be equivalent to the DNA molecule's relationship to the body. Fifteen billion years may be enfolded into us and a deep core memory of all that we will eventually need to know to exist is present at the moment of birth. If so, we are potentially all-knowing. Through a mirroring of the outer and inner worlds, triggered by light and enhanced by our other senses, an unfolding begins. Every moment is a learning event and we are a learning organism. Our interaction with others and with the world is a spontaneous experiment that enchants us and fills us with wonder. The body has the most extraordinary abilities to sense, process, store, retrieve and act. We can describe it but we cannot explain it.

As it moves through space, a subtle transaction exists between the body-mind complex and the world. Everything around us teaches us about the world we create for ourselves. Who we are and who we become are inextricably linked to what we make and inhabit.

Our relationships are conditional. The observer is the observed.
Architecture has become a "third skin."

Synthesis to Distillation

The projects selected for this book cover a period of fifteen years; a full cycle of life experience and expression and half of a generation. The works are products of the same gene pool and reflect certain tendencies, but from the first to the last they represent an evolving world-view and life intentions.

The book begins with the *New Jersey House*, a work that explores formal and spatial propositions within a conceptual framework that sees architecture as a semi-autonomous discipline with its own history, theories, and logic. Our organizational strategies were directed by our curiosities about the notions of order that extend beyond the confines of any particular theory and permeate the whole infrastructure of concepts, ideas, and values. Specifically, we wanted to explore the nature of complexity and our ability to be thrust to the edge where it meets randomness. Our formal interests were focused on a synthesis of diverse elements into a coherent whole. The spaces were abstractly figured and continuous throughout; they had limits but no boundaries.

We still practiced with the belief that architecture gave form to life.

The prelude to this project is *CDLT 1,2,* a house with the same intentions but on a much smaller scale. The difference was primarily in our methodology. For the duration of the project, five years, we worked improvisationally at full size and in real time with "no erasers." If we made a mistake, the rule was to work on it until it looked intentional. We wanted to rediscover the *"Beginners Mind"* of which Suzuki Roshi spoke.

At the back end is *Prairie View.* Architecturally, it is a distillation of components into a coherent whole. It is slow and implosive. The creative sequence begins with the body moving through space and then form, back and forth. It is primarily conceived as a place where design is transparent to experience, and all activities, informal and formal, are seen as a curriculum for learning in the broadest sense. The spatial organization, primarily open and continuous, is intended to promote cooperation rather than competition. *Resistance and interference are the means for creative heat.*

The pivotal projects between the *New Jersey House and Prairie View A&M School of Architecture* are the *Dorland Mountain Art Colony, Carlson Reges Residence, Sinte Gleska University, Forest Refuge, and Warehouse C. Dorland* helped us develop what we call our teaching-practice, a "finishing school" for recently graduated architects. Also, the extreme limits of budget and remote location forced us to make a building with no "body fat." The residential project was a move toward a more straightforward and construction-based logic where intensity of spatial experience took precedence over detailing. This was also the most fluid collaboration with a client to date. From that experience, we now believe that the quality of the architect-client relationship and the architecture are directly proportional.

The University project immersed us into an ancient culture searching for meaning in a contemporary world. This was our first experience with a landscape that was beautiful, vast, and varied; one that could be experienced simultaneously, directly in science and through storytelling. We learned the meaning of a "spiritual landscape." *This project reminded us why we wanted to be architects.*

The Forest Refuge project deeply immersed us into Buddhist practice. This was a necessity for doing what we were asked. We had to merge knowledge and practice by *"living the program,"* discovering through direct experience the middle path, the centerline of gravity, and the stillpoint of a complex and turning world.

We searched for simplicity as it might be on the other side of complexity, one thing nested within another, an implosion,

We began to search for an architecture that moved more slowly in proportion to the cycles, rhythms, and variable speeds of nature and the yogis themselves. The architectural language shifted from a <u>synthesis</u> of articulated elements to a <u>distillation</u> of *"local"* potential *"experiences."* The extent of the unfolding was solely contingent on one's consciousness, at any particular moment in a particular place. *Now, life gave form to architecture.*

In meditation, when the mind is quiet and focused, the body is still and the senses are acute, time and space slowly shift from horizontal to vertical. The yogis in their solitude "go deep" so visual silence is essential. *Warehouse C* was a jump in scale, impacting the core sector of the city, where people, commerce, government, cars, trains, ferry, and ships converged. Because of its size and configuration, we conceived the project as an "urban connector" extending from the city center across a rooftop promenade, the length of the wharf to the ferry terminal with its constant flow of people.

We integrated conventional land and shipbuilding construction techniques and logistics.

All the work with which we are currently engaged, whether it is large-scale planning, small design-build, or buildings for education or prayer, has the social and aesthetic values and code of the recently completed College of Architecture, which is an expression of *"an architecture in slow motion"; a distillation of life giving form to architecture.* The projects for the next fifteen years will continue to emerge out of a continually evolving world view but we expect they will have three things in common: *first, they will be our silent teacher, second, they will be a pretext for our relationships with each other and the world at large, and third they will be vehicles for our quest to make an architecture that recalls the deep imprint of our original pre-conscious experience of unconditional unity.*

As Thomas Merton wrote, "In the midst of a divided world we are called on to be instruments of unity. If we can understand something of ourselves and of others we can begin to share with each other the work of building foundations of spiritual unity. We are already one, but we imagine otherwise. What we have to recover is our original unity. What we have to be is what we are."

The promise of architecture is to help us discover our common ground of being.

Roto Architects began on November 1, 1991, in a complex of historical, industrial buildings in the eastern sector of Los Angeles. Our space is on the top floor of a building in the geographical center of this twenty-acre site. The space has Renaissance proportions. Our two primary views are south and west and the defining geography of flatlands, foothills, and mountains set the growth parameters for Los Angeles.

Clark Stevens and I have worked with many wonderful and talented people to produce a body of work throughout our fifteen-year history. Some of these works are in this book.

Our practice is an open collaboration. All of us, although different in so many ways, have a love of people and architecture in common. The strength of the work has always been in proportion to the affinity we have for each other's differences, and the degree to which we are able to integrate those differences.

I am a teacher who practices architecture and Clark is a naturalist who practices architecture. Although we have worked in interchangeable ways, we are sometimes asked who does what. We answer that Clark works from the ground up and Michael works from the sky down. We meet just above the horizon, the zone of creation as we know it.

Acknowledgments

Although the creative moment is intimate and private, it has heredity. It is the spontaneous convergence of one's interactions and subsequent thoughts that these visions are tested and realized full size by working communally.

There are RoTo people who, over the years, have played a major role in defining and executing the projects. We would like to acknowledge them:

Brian Reiff
Craig Scott
Michael Brandes
Michael Volk
Yusuke Obuchi
Scott Francisco
Jim Bassett
Claudia Montesinos
Carrie Di Fiori
Kirby Smith
Forest Fulton
Sergio Ortiz
Mary Beth Leonard
Pam Romero
Tenzin Thokme
Alyssa Holmquist
John Osborne
Tom Perkins

and those who have been a part of the extended family for years:

Michael Nelms
Katsumi Moroi
Steve Hegedus
and
Bon and Sofia Lyman

Some architects and consultants who have worked with us have also made major contributions, in particular, April Greiman. She has been a design consultant on all of our projects, and has contributed immensely with her insight and unique imagination. Also, John Fisher, Art Yanez, John Ash, Jess Corrigan, and Hirokazu Kosaka.

The open-mindedness and adventurous spirit of certain clients should be noted:

Larry Nicola
David Teiger
Patrick Lannan
Lionel Bordeaux
Sharon Salzberg
Joseph Goldstein
Kathy Reges
Richard Carlson
Hideto Horiike
Lama Gyatso
Lama Zopa
Bruce Raben
Malissa Daniels
Steev Beeson
Des MacAnauf
Linda Duke
Marla Berns
Jacqueline Baas
Mary Jane Jacobs
Yvonne Rand
and
Dr. Ikhlas Sabouni

April Greiman, the designer of this book, committed herself and her staff to this project for the duration and worked closely with RoTo in conceiving and co-editing the book. For many reasons, it would not have happened without her. Roto staff, Alex Pettas, Pam Romero, and Marybeth Leonard were responsible for in-house production.

Farshid Assassi has been our primary photographer for a long time and contributed many of the photos.

The text editors were Aino Paasonen, Aram Saroyan, and especially Linda Hart, who gave us the courage to speak simply.

Eric Owen Moss and Albert Pope each wrote texts that are unique and insightful. We are grateful that they are a part of this project.

David Morton at Rizzoli consulted in a way that gave us the necessary support and encouragement. Also, Douglas Curran, the editor for this book, whose critiques and comments were always understood in the context of the objectives we set at the outset of the process.

To our mentors for their insight and patience.

This is where everything begins, ends, and begins again. It is the point of creation and death, no beginning or end.

Zero is infinity's twin.

It is the point at the center of our being, untouched by extremes, yet embodying their pure essence.

ZERO

Inner and outer worlds unite becoming one. For a moment everything is simultaneous and has equal status, in particular light and matter.

Here there is a perfect balance.
This is no place and
There is no time here.
This is where two become one.

This is the Stillpoint

of a complex and turning world.

Why don't we start our own school?

Did anyone actually say it? Was it a voice we heard in our heads? The thought took us beyond the frustration and anger we felt at our misfortune. The president of Cal Poly Pomona University had removed Ray Kappe as Chair of the School of Architecture—a program Ray had founded three years earlier, in 1969. We were some twenty to twenty-five students whose lives were being wrenched around without any warning by administrators obeying injunctions that American universities in the late sixties sought to enforce. We were meeting twice a week in the evenings, discussing angry strategies of revenge. At least another 125 students shared our concerns.

Why don't we start our own school?

A silence fell over us. A moment before everyone had been talking in a composite of voices full of frustration and urgency. The silence was empty and calming. Suddenly a path had opened to a future that beckoned. It was May, 1972 and SCI-Arc was born.

Cal Poly Pomona's First Architectural Program

Under Kappe's direction, the School of Architecture at Cal Poly Pomona had been young and adventurous. It experimented with curricular and avant-garde approaches to architecture, such as working on projects at scale and full size. It was socially and environmentally aware. A number of us had transferred there, attracted by things we heard and things we had seen. Ray had assembled a young and dynamic faculty with many points of view. All of them seemed to have equal status. We saw no antagonism between them.

The place was a laboratory, a human petrie dish. Students and faculty worked long and productive hours exploring a wide range of ideas and the strategies to implement them. We worked like kids experimenting in the garage or backyard, taking risks without fear of failure. Our process was defined as trial and error. If we hit a dead end, we turned back and went in another direction.

For the first time, we had discovered a life for ourselves. There was no other place we wanted to be. Without realizing it, we were already on a trajectory that was preparing us for the high adventure of creating our own world. We would no longer waste our zeal on trying to change the minds of people who had a different worldview. We would now spend 100% of our time doing what we really needed to do: construct our own school, "the New School." Of the many lessons we learned at this nexus, one of the most important was how anger could be transformed into joy.

1972 was a good year for us, after the darkest period of our young lives, the sixties. Our own revolution was just beginning and we were optimistic about the future, unafraid of the challenges we faced. We didn't know how difficult they would prove to be. We were going to be responsible for our own lives. Each day, we could decide what we wanted to do. We said our comfort level was proportional to our uncertainty. Years later we would reverse our opinion on this. The most significant change for all of us was that we felt empowered to make our own world without having to conform to a preexisting one.

The Formative Sixties

In 1963, the world we had known had changed forever. We had seen President John Kennedy assassinated, the image of his skull shattering was shown on television over and over again, as if the reality of it might be erased the next time. We were in shock. The next phase had just begun, without warning.

In 1968 a series of violent tragedies unfurled:
The Reverend Martin Luther King was assassinated.
University students rioted in Europe and America.
The Vietnam War was building.
Students at Kent State University were killed by police for demonstrating against the war.
The Democratic national convention was the scene for riots and police brutality.
JFK's brother, Robert Kennedy, a presidential candidate, was assassinated.
Marcel Duchamp died.
John Steinbeck died.
Thomas Merton died in Bangkok on Dec 10, the day he had entered the abbey at Gethsemani 27 years before.
Richard Nixon was elected president by the narrowest margin in 100 years.

The conflict between generations had grown exponentially in a decade, and it had hit the streets. My generation came of age in the sixties, as the world we were to inherit fell apart in every way, at all levels, as far as we could see. A new era was beginning but we could not project its future. The world was more than just evolving. We thought of evolution as gradual, sequential and consistent. What we were witnessing was a radical shift. It was a non sequitur as far as we were concerned. We had not been taught to deal with this much change and uncertainty and were unprepared for the upheavals we were experiencing. This was spontaneous combustion or a fire ignited by lightning. It was much bigger than us. The loss of a sense of control was staggering.

Our rights of passage had been brutal and frightening. Yet the more we talked, the more we began to see the wonder that lies within. Maybe life's mysteries were being revealed by this inversion and, if we remained steadfast and non judgmental, we might discover something new about the world and ourselves. If the world was unpredictable, we had to find new things to value and new ways to be. Bob Dylan sang for us, "the times they are a'changing."

In 1969, we knew a moment of optimism as we looked to the sky. On July 21, 1969, Neil Armstrong was the fist human to step on the moon and Apollo 11 then returned safely to earth. The growing quagmire in Vietnam and then Watergate brought us down hard.

"Do joy and pain always come in pairs?" we asked one another.
"The good and the bad, it seemed, are not in opposition, they are two aspects of one thing," Ray told us.

In 1971, the Cal Poly Pomona architecture students and faculty started a velvet revolution.

In 1972, fifty students and faculty left Cal Poly to start their own school. Our motivation was intense. We spent one half of the summer looking for a building, finding a 20,000 sq. ft. warehouse at 1800 Berkeley Street, in Santa Monica, and the other half turning it into a laboratory for our work. In one year the community was to grow to a hundred.

In 1972, Richard Nixon was re-elected by a landslide, as the events of Watergate were beginning to unfold.

Belief and disbelief seemed to come in equal doses. Life was, apparently, a zero sum game. We accepted it without complaining. After all we were on an adventure and there were always hardships. Life was a pilgrimage.

Life at "The New School"

Potluck dinners brought us together over food, all-school meetings brought us together over issues, presenting our projects brought us together over ideas, and work parties to improve our building brought us together over construction. We seemed to spend as much time together as we did alone, constantly trying to understand our roles and responsibilities to others and ourselves.

At first, SCI-Arc avoided conventional institutional structures. There were no "professors," just students with various interests. There were no classes, no curriculum, no central administration, no assigned spaces. We set up our own place to work. Each one of us would decide what we wanted to do, based on our own curiosities, as long as we contributed to the general debate which was as much social as architectural. The main rule was that we had to participate in the "family life" of the school.

We were constantly trying to understand our roles and responsibilities to others and ourselves. We negotiated everything. The rules of engagement were being invented from moment to moment, and if they worked we remembered them. If not, we modified them and moved on. Things were open and fluid. Confusion led to conflict, which led to creative dialogue and action. We accepted all of this without hesitation. We thrived on it. Later we would realize the great advantages of being young and inexperienced. We worked all of the time. We all grew close. There was nothing else we wanted to do and no other place we wanted to be.

The biggest challenges were twofold: knowing how to take full responsibility for our own lives, and how to be an active part of a community that was simultaneously defining itself. Change was constant and continuous. Previously, parents and teachers had done most of the work for us. We realized that responsibility required experience. We re-read John Dewey, which had a huge influence on the concept and structure of teaching and learning practices at the school from that time to the present.

Theoretical Aspects of Our Educational Practice

The school, in all its confusion and good intentions was our first great teacher. Science defines this type of free-for-all as "self-organizing." The relationships between each of us and the environment that was emerging were mutually defining.

It was also autocatalytic. Everyone was experiencing the same feelings of confusion, hope, fear, joy, anger, elation, jealousy, respect, fatigue, and excitement. We were all on the same life boat. We developed affinities for each other's differences, knowing that our diversity made us a more complex and stronger organism. We depended on one another. It was not only a necessity, we came to the awareness that we wanted it that way. We had become a tribe.

What we knew least about was the history and theories of constructing an alternative education practice, which is what we were doing. After four months of discussions, and debates that came out of the big question we asked in so many ways "What is SCI-Arc, and what is our role in this community?" I decided that one way to answer the question was to take it on as a creative design problem. I would try to design the school we were trying to manifest. The next question I was compelled to ask was "Who else had worked on the problem of alternative education?"

As I did my research, I began to see familiar patterns and recurring themes—three in particular. First, there was the relationship of freedom to structure. We had convinced ourselves that they were in conflict. We were wrong. They were two aspects of one thing: life. The issue was one of balance. This is always the issue.

Second, there was the nature of change: types of change, rates of change, and frequency of change.

Third, there was the relationship of part to whole. Each part had to have an imprint of the purpose of the whole system, an internal logic that would set its performance criteria and establish limits as well as the discretion to assess and respond to unexpected new conditions. Everything at all scales is interconnected and interdependent. I re-read The Federalist Papers, in which James Madison makes a clear and convincing argument about the necessity for giving equal weight to individual rights and communal responsibility. This is what all of us in the SCI-Arc community had to come to terms with.

We had to see the whole thing.
We had to think systemically.
We had to see the value of interdependence.

The year SCI-Arc was born we were enthusiastic about starting a new school.

We were motivated by the idea that this might be possible.

We knew that it would be a creative process in which we would learn about ourselves and each other.

We experienced fear and conflict but sensed that this was a positive thing, an inherent part of the process. Most importantly, we learned what it meant to be a collection of individuals coalescing into a community, aware of the uncertainties of change and the belief that it would make our lives and, in turn, the world better. I've thought and said, SCI-Arc is the story Lord of the Flies *with a good ending.*

Change and uncertainty were our new medium We were living it. They were not conceptual but real.

The school was THE GRAND EXPERIMENT. It was THE PROJECT.

Our words and ideas were tested almost immediately, at every moment.

Every day our survival was contingent on our ability to be open to possibilities.

Why were we doing this? What would we achieve? What would our payback be? What were our guarantees for success? We did not know, but one thing we knew: IT WAS THE RIGHT THING TO DO.

It was a time of:
1 boundless optimism
2 extreme motivation
3 intense conflict
4 great learning and
5 immense fun

How could this be?
How could our comfort level be equal to the uncertainty?
What gave us the strength to move forward?
Our faith in the COSMIC MIND.
The experience of renewal and rebirth was almost as familiar as our own heartbeat.
We were experiencing the ACT OF CREATION itself.
SCI-Arc grew and learned.
Like any organism, its evolution was influenced by its parts—all of the individuals that made it up.

People were the MOLECULES and SCI-Arc was the BODY.

It finally stood erect and took its place in the world and spoke to anyone who would listen.

It was a place of freedom, a place where people could invent a LIFE that was uniquely theirs. It taught us, by example, that anything imaginable was possible. The fact that it existed, was evidence of what is possible with FAITH.

SCI-Arc not only talked about change, it has lived it. Walked the talk. And in the spirit of its first moment of life, it has always been willing to engage the world as it is, in an unconditional relationship.

SCI-Arc is a complete invention, constructed full size, in real time. The ultimate collective thesis project expressing the ideas of people with strong wills, who believe it is their mission to change the world in constructive ways.

SCI-Arc encouraged us to live the life we want to create for others.

SCI-Arc was the first place we could imagine the world as we wanted it to be and would try to make it. We were convinced that the best way to test an idea was to build it as close as we could to the ideal. We knew this was as close as we would ever get to the ideal. Knowing what was possible was the motivation to do it again and again and again and again, until it was time to go.

SCI-Arc is both a particle and a wave.

The making of this house attempts to close the gap between the moments of conception and occupation.

No working drawings were made. Sketches were produced for the carpenter to work from each morning.

New ideas were tested full-size without erasers.

project_
date_   cdlt 1,2
    1987–1992

location_   los angeles, ca   **cdlt 1,2**

client_   rotondi family

project team_   michael rotondi
    benedetto rotondi
    read miller

structural
engineer_
    gordon polon

builder_   michael rotondi

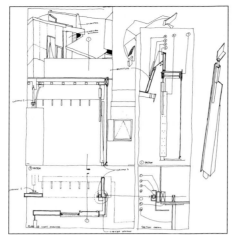

words :

conjugation

hybrid

composite structure

reciprocity

process

systematic

circumstantial

improvisation

exactitude

spontaneity

CDLT 1,2

house resulted from an interest in working at full scale, improvisationally, and closing the gap between the moments of conception and inhabitation. The ideas, rather than being speculative as when first drawn, came out of the direct experience of testing ideas immediately by building them. We made no working drawings for this project. Instead, we produced sketches from which the contractor worked each day. At the end of the day, the contractor left lights pointed at areas that needed resolution.

The manner of working expanded and contracted simultaneously. The scale of the project and the fact that we were our own clients made it possible to unite idea and construction. Each component became the impetus for the next idea. Nothing was subtracted; rather than intertwining layers, we added each layer to the next. The advantage is being able to live what one thinks and feels. We decided that no "eraser" would be used with this house, literally or figuratively. Instead of an idea merely feeding on itself as a kind of abstraction, it was constructed, and the next idea came out of looking at or feeling the consequences of the previous decision.

A rule-based system served two purposes. It provided a structure for all the decisions that would be made over a five-year period, ensuring that there would be some level of coherence. The rules also conveyed information about ideas or techniques to the builder and back again to the architect. The most obvious rules concerned the geometric order in plan and section. We established a hierarchy of materials that was used in a very strict way, and the size and type of materials were determined by their functions.

The builder had degrees in literature and music composition so we were able to discuss with him, in the abstract, the rhythmic nature of ordering systems and how they operate as a less than visible structure for spontaneity. These discussions created a frame of reference for his decisions and he often sought a visual equivalent for musical concepts and notation. The house was a constructed, daily journal: conceptual fingerprints over the entire building recording, through its body language, its creation.

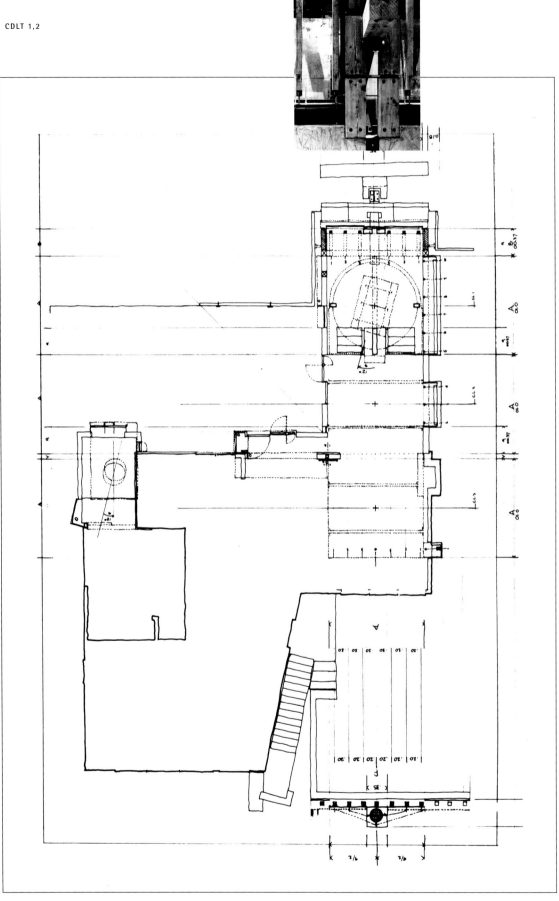

1987   *Standing in the grand hall of the Banca di Verona was the best place to pause and look back. I had just walked the entire building with Arrigo Rudi, longtime collaborator of Carlo Scarpa, the architect who had been commissioned to design the bank. Over a five-year period, Scarpa and Rudi worked continuously on the project that was now finally complete. Five years of creativity and construction in a continuous feedback loop!*

The project had begun in the usual way: the first sketch was pure intuition, then a more precise drawing and a model. From that point on, the process was atypical. They worked at scale through drawings and models, defining the scope and function as an aesthetic emerged. Over and over, the process would be generative, analytical and critical, then back again, eventually reaching a phase of refinement and detail. When the creative work was complete, construction began. From that point on, decisions, relatively minor compared to the earlier phases of work, were practical and technical. The architect was expected to make periodic visits to the site to observe and clarify. Why, then, had it taken five years?

Thom Mayne and I built experimental houses in Venice, California, working with young builders, some of whom had been our students at SCI-Arc. We were adventurous enough then to not have figured everything out in advance. We designed as we went along. Since there had been many iterations of models and drawings, by the time construction began, most of the design work was done. We still made changes as we went along, using the building as our full-size model.

As familiar as these projects of Scarpa's in Verona felt to me, there was something about them that was intriguingly elusive. Over the next few months, I was able to visit his other projects in the Veneto region and I began to develop a sense of what was different in his work, besides his obvious aesthetic predilections.

Scarpa's work had a body language bearing a clear trace of his conceptual fingerprints. For me, this was a completely unexpected way to think of a building. Didn't other buildings have body language? Perhaps, but these were distinct. These buildings were a visible record of all that they had gone through in coming into the world. They held the memory of the creative process, particularly that of their relationship with the architect.

I had been told that Scarpa would begin construction before the drawings were complete, while design continued on a parallel track. Each idea was tested full-size in real time, then became the impetus for the next set of ideas. The building, the architect, and the builders were all in a special dance with moves that mostly remained embodied in the building. This could be sensed. My body recognized it.

This way of working was freer than any other I knew. It was also risky. What if you did not like what you had done the day before? What if all the decisions did not add up and the whole became incoherent? It was like a chess game that needed basic rules to guide the process without restricting it. In concept, this was how we worked in the studio, but if we did not like what we had just done, we had erasers and more cardboard. Working full-size meant no second chance. I wanted to make a building using this process. I wanted to test myself.

After touring Italy for eight weeks, I spent the next eight weeks at SCI-Arc's villa in the Ticinese portion of the Southern Alps, overlooking Lake Lugano. I studied my sketchbooks, and thought about this type of praxis—completely free from conventional working methods and sequences. How could the work remain coherent as a system, aesthetically and linguistically? I'd read as a student that architecture, like other human expressions, was a language and must be conceived and executed with the intent of communicating to others in an articulate way. It needed a "grammar" and rules. However, if an open-ended, spontaneous approach were taken, rules would undermine the process. But maybe not. I recalled that we had had the same concerns in the early days of SCI-Arc. Without knowing it, we had been embedded in a self-organizing system guided by rules that naturally emerged over time. If we paid attention and remained open to the possibility of changing our minds in light of new experiences, then we might be able to keep it both working and consistent. Now I know that everything has an internal logic that provides structure, as all the parts interact in apparently spontaneous ways. Pay attention and let it be.

Maybe a building had a DNA. I wondered, is it possible that freedom and structure are nested within each other? I've come to know this to be true.

Back from my four-month sabbatical, I settled in for a few weeks and then began to work in this way on my family house in Los Angeles, with a carpenter and his two assistants and with my ten-year-old son. We worked off-and-on over the next five years. There were no construction drawings, just sketches and a few drawings that set down the ordering and dimensional system for the surface and volumes.

The system was linear, circular, and sequential, all of which we embedded in the finished concrete slab for reference, if needed. The carpenter would build what was sketched. If it were unclear to him, he'd move on to some other part of the project and place lights on the areas that needed attention. When I returned home, usually after dark, long after they had left, I would turn on the lights and sit looking at the building, then sketch what was needed to keep them going the next day. If there were a "mistake," we would work on it until it became intentional. Basically, there were no mistakes and no erasers. I discovered the relationship between freedom and fear.

Throughout the entire process, I was interested in my son's ideas, which I knew would be fresh and radical, due to his inexperience. Not limited by prior knowledge, he would say things that I would not even have allowed myself to think. Working with a young, growing person showed me how we limit ourselves as we get more experienced. I began to remember things I had once known and ways I used to be. I rediscovered, in him, the deep intelligence of innocence. "Beginner's mind" believes that anything imaginable is possible. Shunryu Suzuki wrote in Zen Mind Beginner's Mind, "In the beginner's mind there are many possibilities, but in the expert's mind there are few."

"Dad, can my bedroom be like a tree-house?
Dad, can the entire front wall of the room be glass and slide out of the way so I am sleeping out of doors?
Dad, can we put a big opening in the roof and make a big telescope so I can see the stars at night when I am lying down, like the stars of my birthday constellation?
Dad, can we make the concrete walls look like your photographs of the desert from the airplane?"

My first thought was always "that's not possible," but I would keep it to myself and, with some patience and drawing, I discovered that it was possible to accomplish what he suggested. Next, I would have to confront my ego, realizing once again that these were his ideas and I wanted them to be mine. How absurd was my need to be first and original? Who had given me that imprint? What better teacher to have and what better time to let go? Things began to change for me. I learned a lot from him and still do. He made me a better teacher.

I eventually stopped working on the house, and left it incomplete when I moved to another house nearby, but my son asked if he could stay in the unfinished house. I gave him a list of items to be completed and told him that the house would be his if he finished it. He eventually completed the work and added a few new features of his own. The house is now his home.

They asked if we could replace the cottage that burned for $39,000.

Could we conceive of it as a cave and a tent?

Could we fill it with the maximum amount of light?

Was it possible to make it by hand without electricity?

We said yes.

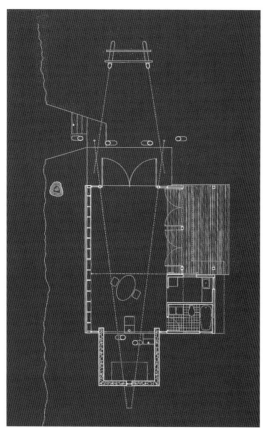 

dorland mountain arts colony

project_	
date_	dorland mountain arts colony 1993–1994
location_	temecula, ca
client_	dorland mountain arts colony

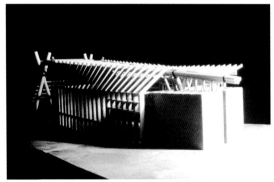

The Dorland Mountain Arts Colony, established in 1979, covers approximately ten acres of a 300-acre Nature Conservancy preserve overlooking the Temecula Valley in California. A central live oak grove, two spring-fed ponds, and a variety of plant, bird and animal life inhabit the site.

In 1992, an accidental fire burned down the Colony's Lake Cottage. We donated design-build services to replace the 1,000 square foot cabin on a budget of $30,000. Writers, composers and visual artists come to Dorland Mountain Arts Colony for retreat, reflection and work. It is a place of solitude and transition.

There is no electricity on the site so residents plan their daily routines according to available light. They reconnect with natural systems and circadian rhythms not always evident in urban environments. The cabin has two modes that respond to its Savannah-like environment—one open, light-gathering and breeze-capturing; the other, a shuttered insulating mode that responds to the cool, high-desert nights. Screen and shutter systems are used in place of large glass surfaces resulting in economic benefits and an increased sense of physical well-being.

We designed a "tent" for working and a "cave" for sleeping using wood, lumber and lodge poles, concrete, steel cable and strap and fabric for the light-providing roof. The size of individual elements was determined by the capacity of two people to lift them into place.

The only heating element, a wood-burning stove, is adjacent to the spaces used in the evening and early morning. These spaces benefit from solar heat radiating from massive stone and concrete walls in the sleeping area. Daylight is augmented with a wide strip of polyester fabric running the length of the cabin. Although inexpensive, this fabric provides substantial heat reflectance while allowing natural light into the rooms. Shaded exterior areas extend the interior studio space and open to views of the Temecula Valley through a canopy of live oaks.

project_ date_	dorland mountain arts colony 1993–1994
location_	temecula, ca
client_	dorland mountain arts colony
project team_	michael rotondi, clark stevens, yusuke obuchi, scott francisco, jonathan winton, angela hiltz, jim bassett
assistants_	brian reiff, jin kim, kenneth kim, tracy loeffler, geoff lynch, caroline spigelski, joy stingone, michael yeo
color + design consultant_	april greiman
structural engineer_	joseph perazzeli
builder_	roto architects

Nicola

is a 100-seat restaurant and food service operation in a 52-story high-rise building in downtown Los Angeles. The cuisine is "contemporary food with ethnic influences." The public dining area, located on the ground floor, is divided between a 1700-sq.-ft. interior space (including rest rooms, kitchen, and service areas) and a six-story high glass enclosed atrium space of 900 sq. ft.

The design is a result of discovering and constructing ordering systems that are both latent and deliberate in the existing conditions and programmatic requirements. The restaurant, although divided into areas such as kitchen, service, bar, waiting/entry, rest rooms, and both interior and exterior dining areas, is unified through the geometry of organization and constructed systems. Initially, a map was derived that laid out the principal ordering systems that would describe the characteristics of the place (functional and spatial).

Then, through the experimental use of woodwork, metal, stone and drywall, the space was given form based on the geometry of the ordering map and imagining the movement of the body through space. The objective was to create conceptual and perceptual unity.

A significant part of design at RoTo involves the collaboration of people in other creative fields. In the case of Nicola, the collaboration with a graphic designer for color and material finishes and an industrial designer for lighting elements strengthened and expanded the design concept.

In nature, complex systems are layered interdependently resulting in fundamental beauty. Discovering this principle existing in architecture is the most significant experience at Nicola.

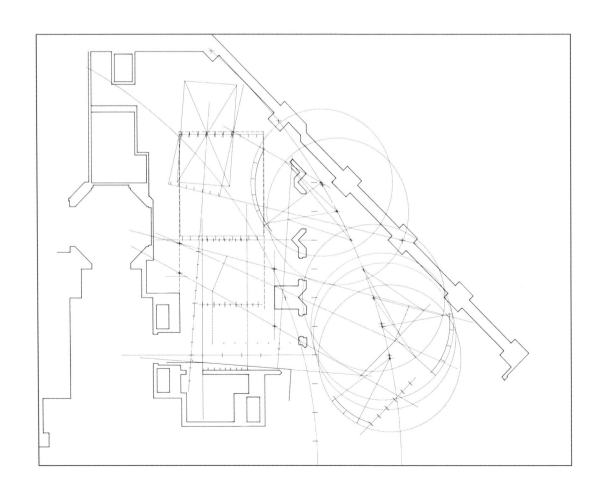

nicola
restaurant

project_
date_   nicola restaurant
               1993
location_   los angeles, ca
client_   larry nicola

nicola restaurant

project_	nicola restaurant
date_	1993
location_	los angeles, ca
client_	larry nicola
project team_	michael rotondi, clark stevens, brian rieff, angela hiltz, gregory kight, jason king, milana kosovac, yusuke obuchi, scott williams
color + design graphics consultant_	april greiman
structural engineer_	joseph perazzelli
m/e/p engineer_	(m)mb&a, (e) g&w consultants
general contractor_	rotondi construction john rotondi

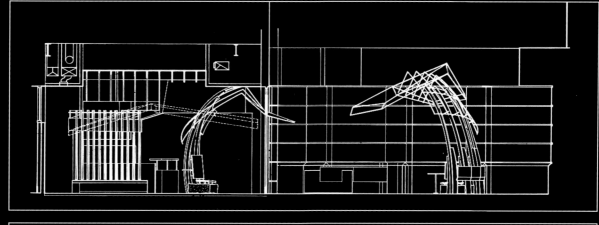
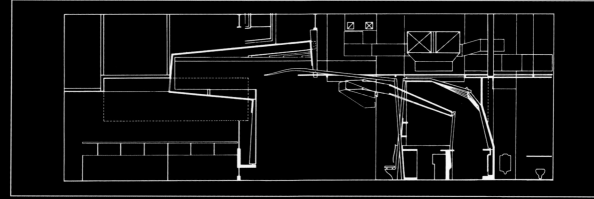

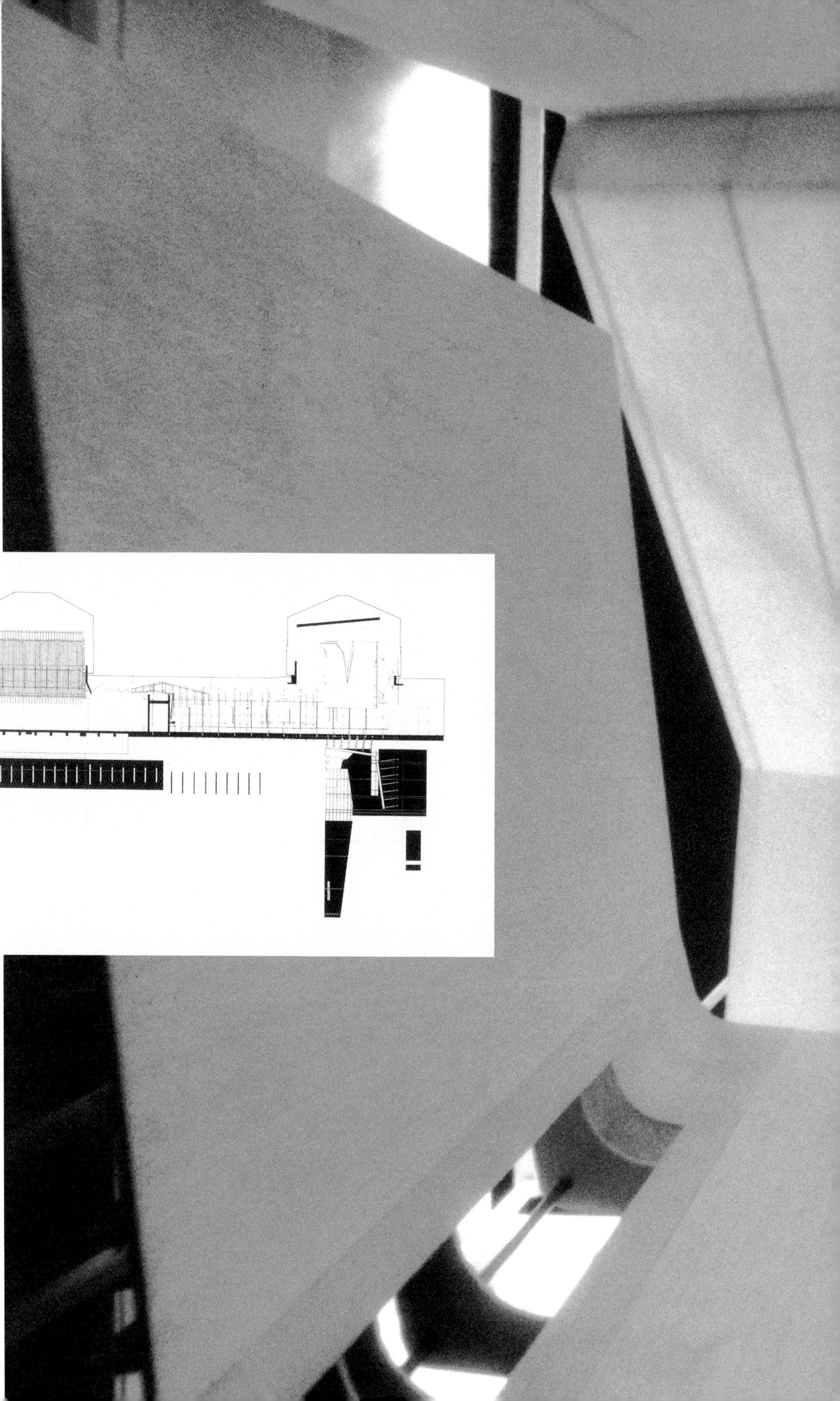

circolo restaurant

project_ date_	circolo restaurant 1991
location_	glendale, ca
client_	circolo, llc
project team_	michael rotondi, theresa ross, francisco gutierrez, gregory kight
structural engineer_	joseph perazelli
electrical engineer_	saul goldin & associates
mechanical engineer_	mb&ta
general contractor_	rotondi construction john rotondi

Circolo Restaurant

is sited within a new building that seemed medieval in its lack of control and order. Our geometric analysis of the building identified misalignments and offsets that we decided to "correct" with the placement of new elements. The existing spaces were two shifted rectilinear volumes, each punctuated by a big vertical space.

Three types of Italian dining for three speeds have been combined within the restaurant: a cafe bar and deli for espresso, snacks, and take-away, tavolo caldo (with food that has been prepared in advance) and the trattoria, for the long meal. One of the tall spaces was to have a 30-ft.-high pizza altar, as a tribute to Carmine, a great chef in L.A.

We used wood as the primary material. Inspiration came from the beauty of Russian wooden buildings, Japanese wooden temples, and Scandinavian wooden boats. We also admired unfinished wood-framed buildings. Working directly with a crew of craftsmen, we applied the following operations on the material: repetition, rotation, bending, shifting and extension. The simple device of points and lines was used to imply planes and volumes.

This project was the precursor to Nicola.

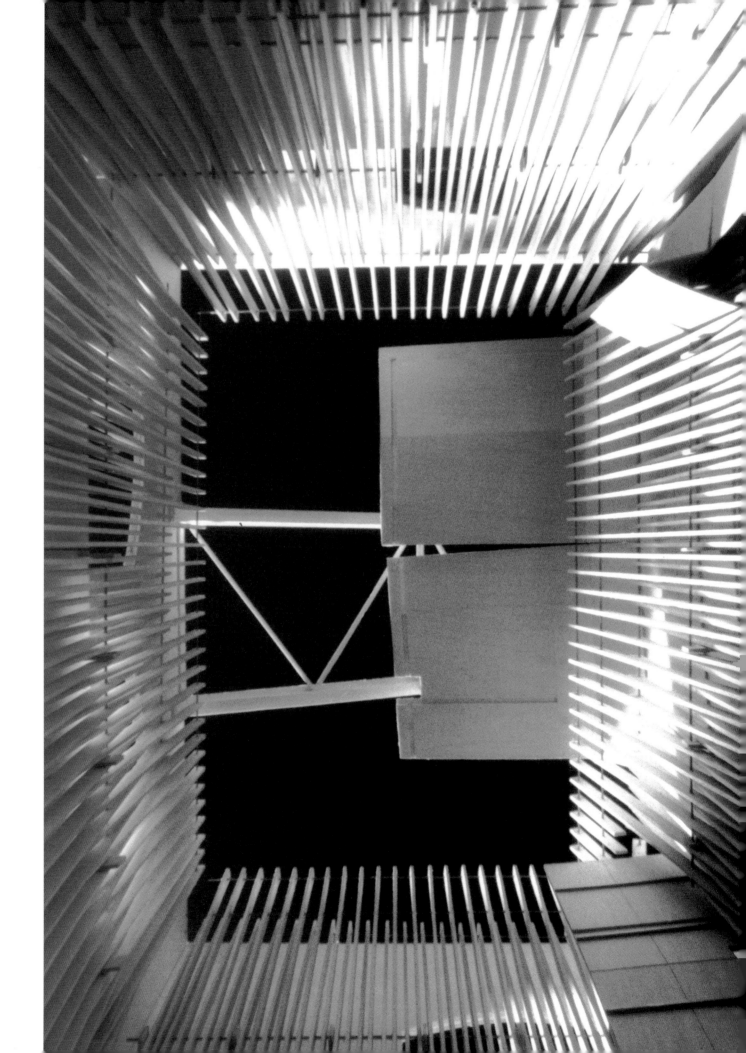

new jersey
house

project_ date_	new jersey house 1990–1996
location_	bernardsville, new jersey
client_	david tieger

He wanted a house that felt traditional but looked contemporary. Spatially it reflected his interests in exploring complex models that are applied to human organizations.

New Jersey House

is on a large and very special site. This area of the state is semi-rural with large grasslands dispersed within a seemingly continuous forest. The site is situated on a knoll that is both forest and field, sloping downward into a valley that extends for thirty miles. The house is designed to experience all of this. At the end of a long driveway, extending from the street through the forest at the edge of the field, is an entry-motor court shaped by a building and trees. The L-shaped plan consists of an east-to-west private wing and a north-to-south semi-private zone that includes a media center, small garden and guest room, all of which are adjacent to a long swimming pool. These two zones pass through each other like interfering magnetic fields, creating a third zone for family living and dining areas and library. Although many of the activities have distinctly bounded areas, the entire inner space of the building is fluid; one space becomes another throughout. All the main areas are contiguous and easily accessible to outside spaces made into decks, patio, porch, garden and pool. From the project's inception, we explored different ways of incorporating the client's interests pertaining to concepts of dynamic human organizations as described in 3-D diagrams. The ordering systems we devised through the drawing and subsequent modeling were linear and incremental with frequencies and phasing that worked in plan and section at once.

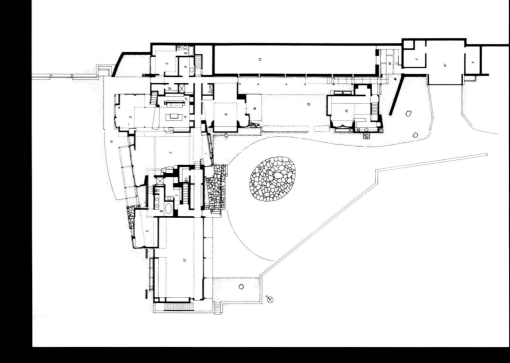

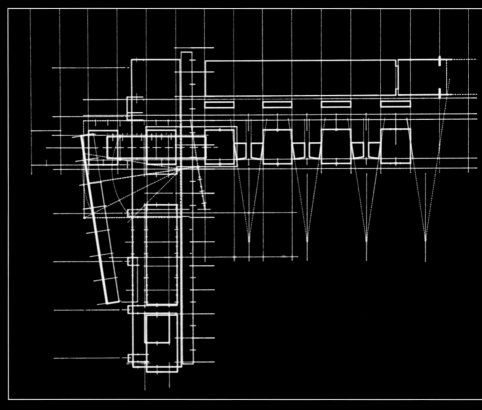

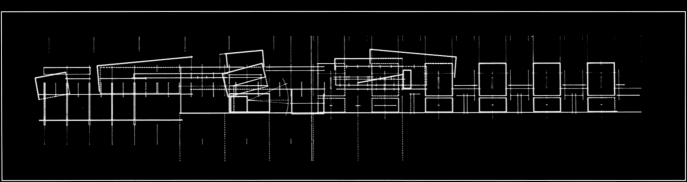

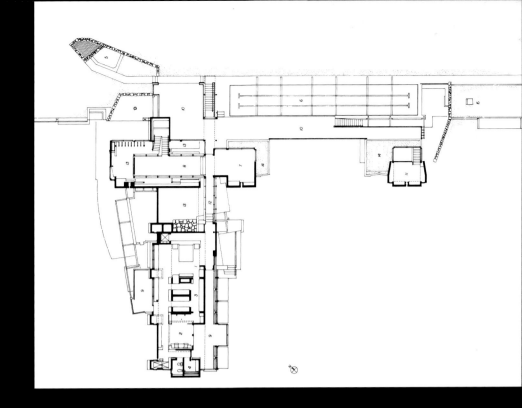

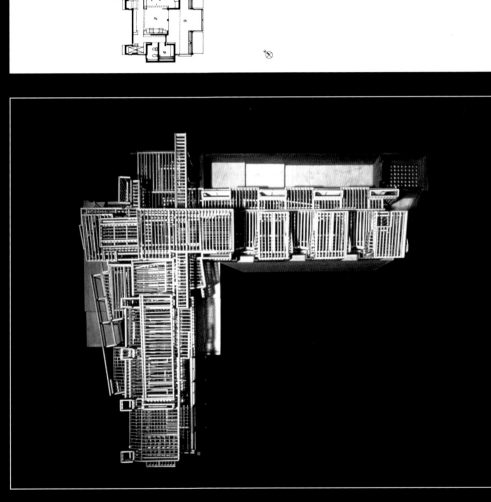

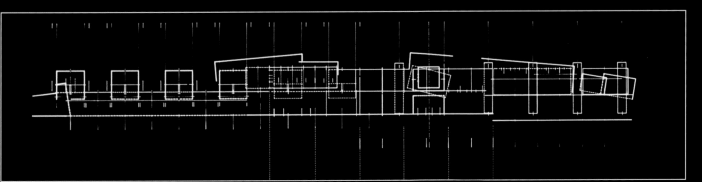

new jersey house

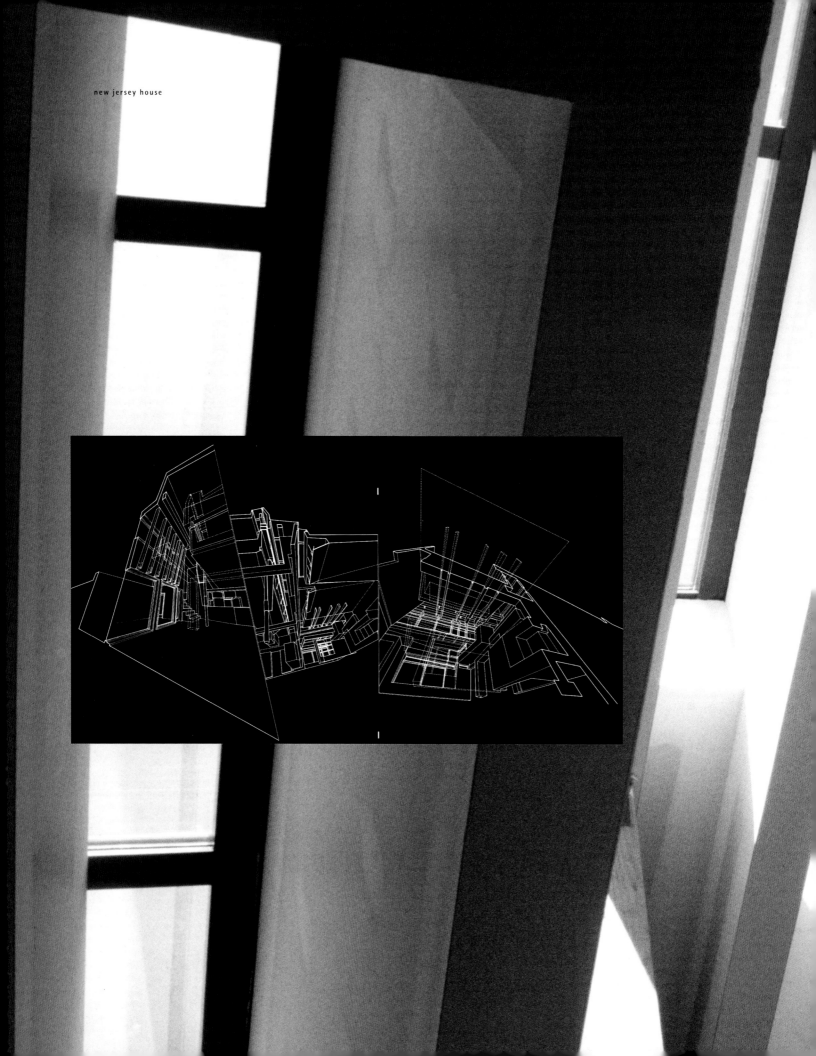

familiar to my body and unfamiliar to my eyes

project_ date_	new jersey house 1990–1996
location_	bernardsville, new jersey
client_	david tieger
project team_	michael rotondi, clark stevens
assistants_	michael brandes, brian reiff, craig scott rebecca bearss, francisco gutierrez, lisa iwamoto, kenneth kim, tracy loeffler, donato maselli, stuart spafford
landscape architect_	walter c. carroll, jr., inc.
design consultant_	chermayeff & geismar, inc.
structural engineer_	joseph perazzelli
civil engineer_	gladstone design, inc.
m/e/p engineer_	mb&a
general contractor_	f.j. korfmann contracting, inc.

Can we design a house that seems quite familiar to my body and unfamiliar to my eyes?

David greeted me at Newark Airport. I needed to know how he lived in order to imagine the house I would design for him, a house that would be a medium for his life. I asked what he wanted the house to be like. His answer seemed like a Zen koan. "Can we design a house that seems familiar to my body and unfamiliar to my eyes?" He was more concerned with performance than with a look or a style. It was as if he were saying, "In this house I want my body to be perfectly at ease, while what I see will continually challenge me with unknown possibilities."

Can something be simultaneously both strange and familiar?

I had never been asked such a question. I was startled and puzzled. I hesitated, but my body answered yes. Searching for an answer started me on an endless quest. There would undoubtedly be many answers, all of them correct. David and I spent the next two days talking, diagramming and sketching.

I first met David in Los Angeles where he had come for a business meeting. Our mutual friend, Warren, who had been mentoring me for two years, introduced us. Warren was a teacher in the broadest sense and a sociologist by training. He had been an educator, university president, advisor to presidents and was now developing a leadership institute at USC. Six times annually for six hours, twenty-five corporate and institutional executives met in Los Angeles for intense, open-ended discussions focused on theories concerning the intended functions and performance of social infrastructures within corporations. Any and all human organizations were considered to be learning organisms.

The anatomy of a company—seen as a dynamic learning organism—was a new concept to corporate America. It was the thesis of a book written by Tom Peters, Managing on the Edge of Chaos, *which Warren had given me to read. This was one of the accepted models for the executives at these meetings. Their frame of reference was inevitable change. The question was not how change should be managed, but rather how it could best be embraced.*

What kind of company do you run, how is it organized and for what purpose?

My mother used to ask, "What's the big idea?" In essence, this is what I asked David when we met. I was curious about how he visualized his company and how vividly he could describe it. What was his ratio of left to right brain thinking? His thinking was very spatial, moving easily between different points of view. He described the entire organization of his company systemically.

The "big idea" was encoded like DNA embedded deep in the structure of the organization and it effectively and invisibly set limits for everything that moved and changed. Parts were considered in relation to the whole, all were dynamic and fluid. One could override this autonomic system in response to new information that would affect things in unexpected ways.

In New Jersey, as David talked to me, I diagrammed various states of order with linear and incremental points and lines, in fits and starts, as if a pause button now and then interrupted emerging and changing systems of people and ideas. Questions the RoTo crew and I faced over the next five years were: How can we spatialize this? What is the architectural equivalent? Is it possible to conceive of a building analogically similar to a company in terms of a dynamic system of parts in relation to the whole, a building also responsive to the next order of magnitude present on the site and beyond?

Spatial and conceptual coherence became the critical issues. The house would seem familiar; yet challenge the eye with strangeness. David's original question became our golden rule. The house would be complex and coherent, engaging and inviting to the mind and the body.

We worked on the house for five years. David enjoyed the creative process as much as we did, wanting to test almost every idea before it might be edited out. Sometimes these tests were full-size. The results were always surprising and inevitable.

The body never lies. When David finally moved in, he smiled and said, "It works!"

END

gemini consulting's learning center

project_	gemini consulting's learning center
date_	1993
location_	morristown, nj
client_	gemini consulting
	david teiger

Gemini Consulting's Learning Center in New Jersey was built for an international business consulting group. We envisioned an exploratorium for adults that would promote the development and exploration of new ideas and ways of thinking about the world and its socioeconomic structure. Our shared objective was to construct the architectural equivalent of the company's guiding principles. We framed and shaped our architectural concepts around the ideas of collaboration, dynamic systems and structures and transformative processes.

Our early discussions with Gemini led to some working assumptions: young people learn directly from the world; initially their imaginations are both spacious and spatial. As they mature, their thinking becomes more compartmentalized, two-dimensional and static, as do the environments in which they learn, live and work. Play, which is the primary mode for structured and circumstantial learning for children, is often considered unacceptable for working adults. In contrast, we recognize that adult imaginative play is essential to developing the best ideas in any organization. Together, the RoTo and Gemini teams created the physical and intellectual models that became the Learning Center. The space is both segmented and fluid in all directions. The Learning Center, conceived as a prototype for future centers, provides a variety of places in which to play/work, seriously and otherwise.

Facilitating communication is critical to the success of the Learning Center. In our design, we incorporated a number of ways to encourage communication, from low tech to high tech solutions. For example, there is a blackboard in the public spaces for people to leave notes or equations for others to comment upon. The Center also has state-of-the-art communications equipment such as video conferencing and computers.

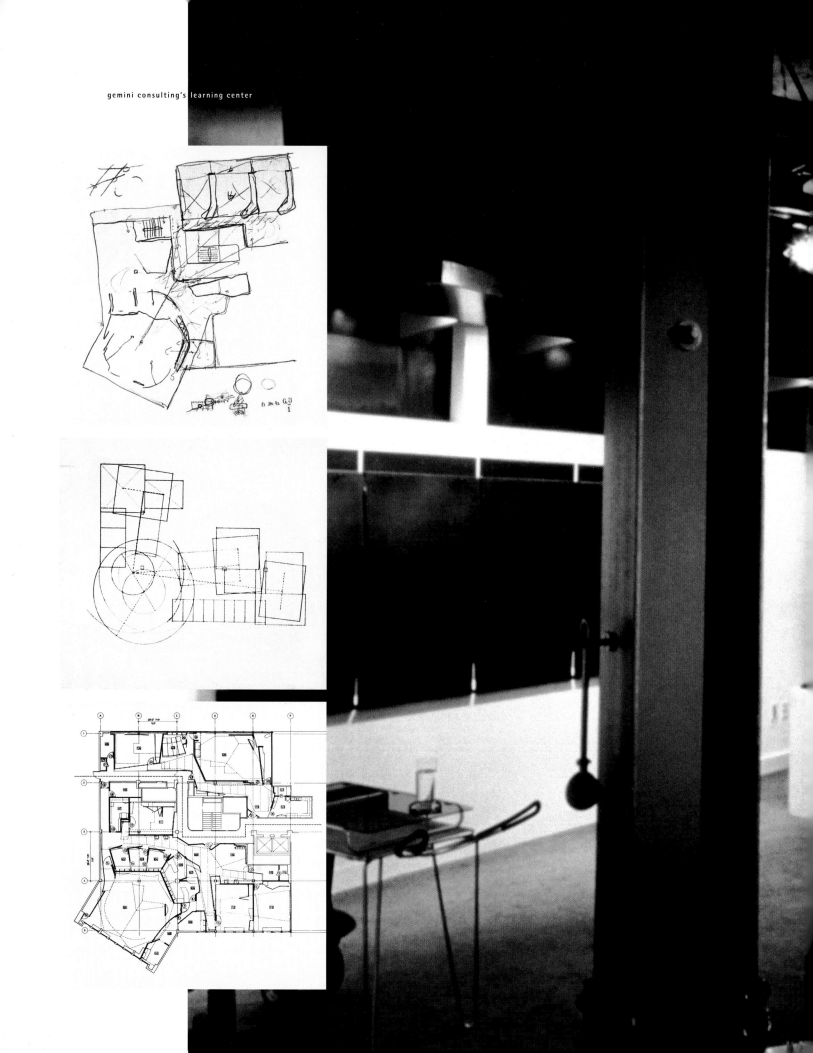

project_ date_	gemini consulting's learning center 1993
location_	morristown, nj
client_	gemini consulting david teiger
project team_	michael rotondi, clark stevens, brian rieff, craig scott, tracy loeffler
assistants_	michael brandes, max massie richard kasemsarn, jason king, milana kosovac, yusuke obuchi
graphics_	chermayeff + geismar
design consultant_	kay kollar design
m/e/p engineer_	mb&a
general contractor_	clearcut construction

This was like a fictional project for our students.

The house is for a couple—he is an urban industrial recycler and builder, she is an art collector.

They have a kennel with thirty world-class show dogs on a twenty-acre industrial site.

carlson-reges house

project_
date_
    carlson-reges house
    1992–1996
location_
    los angeles, ca
client_
    richard carlson + kathy reges

The/Wall

The first questions that Richard asked after our introductions were, "How would you eliminate the intense southern sun entering and heating up the inside of the building and how would you alleviate the ambient sound and diesel fumes from the trains?"

Richard was a problem solver. The bigger the problem, the greater his enjoyment. He was also pragmatic, preferring solutions that were obvious and clever.

When described, Kathy and Richard sounded more like the fictional clients we invent for our students.

- *They collected the work of emerging artists to help support them.*
- *They had a kennel filled with world-class show dogs.*
- *They were the godparents and impresarios of the Brewery, an industrial complex transformed into an arts district.*
- *He was an industrial building recycler and had large stores of heavy construction material and the heavy equipment to move it around.*
- *He was a builder.*
- *She was an arts culture visionary in Los Angeles.*
- *They were both inspiring and fearless.*

Richard and Kathy had master planned the Brewery, the largest live-work artist-in-residence complex in Los Angeles. A population of 600 lived and/or worked on 24 acres. We had moved our office there in 1991.

For Clark and I, the obvious answer to Richard's questions was to build a detached wall 60 feet high and 60 feet wide, thereby solving the problems of sun, sound and smell. Richard immediately agreed. The most obvious was sometimes the most unusual. This was the first of many questions.

carlson-reges house

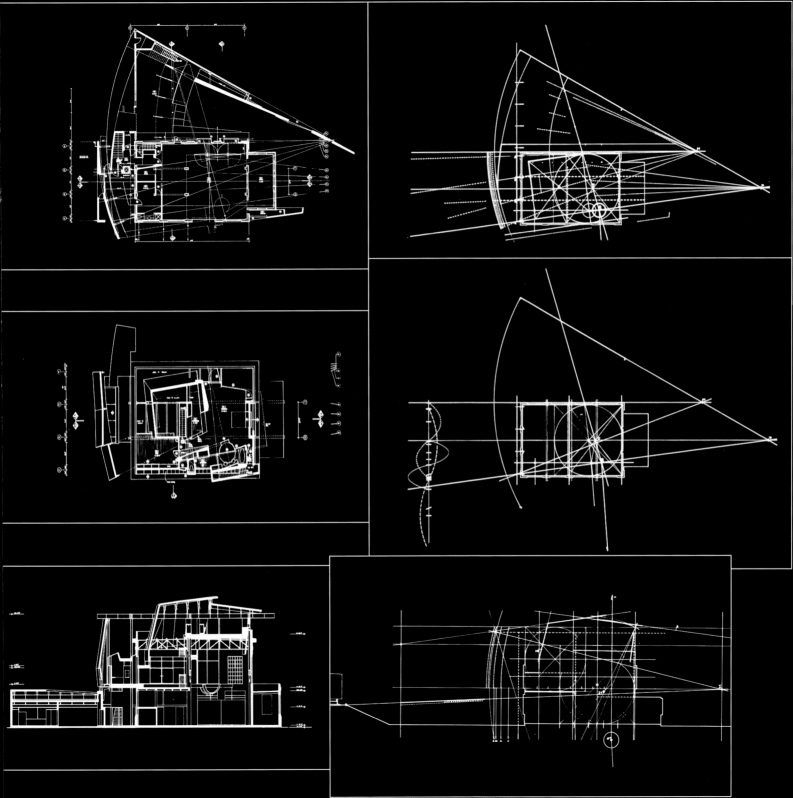

The Pool

We decided to have a swimming pool, but we want to preserve the garden," said Kathy during one of our meetings. The main living area was on the second level, 16 feet above the garden. The ground floor was for the kennel, guestroom, kennel offices and art space, rainforest—a pity to interrupt it all.

Clark and I looked at each other and nodded. If the pool was one level up (+16 ft.), it would be adjacent to the living area and while swimming you would see the city when coming up for air. The practical benefits will be a full size, shaded garden that gets watered when the water spills over the sides of the pool above. Richard smiled and said, "Practical and obvious." "But how do we make it and hold it up,?" we all asked at once. We can use the empty gas storage tanks, an 8 ft. diameter, 20 ft. high cylindrical tank can be sliced vertically in half, and both halves put together will make a 40 ft.span over the garden, just right.

They never once disregarded a potential answer to a problem, no matter how unusual. The process was one of improvisation; anything said was accepted and the basis for the next thing said, and eventually tested by building it. There was no going back and no erasers. The house became a record of our relationship.

carlson-reges house

was built with materials from the owners' salvage yard. We worked together improvisationally and opportunistically within a pre-established spatial framework.

One of the clients is a builder; the other breeds and trains show dogs and is active in the Los Angeles Arts community. They have lived for some time in what was once an electric company cabling structure north of downtown Los Angeles. The stripped classical concrete and steel structure is surrounded by a yard containing a collection of building materials and industrial artifacts collected from two generations of work and urban renovation. During that time, the client/builder and his family acquired considerable skill and experience in the renovation of large-scaled industrial structures but before this project, had not collaborated with an architect.

The clients requested that their expanding collection of paintings and sculptures be accommodated to allow for occasional public showings, while preserving the privacy of their living space. The design addresses the acoustic and environmental problems associated with living in a large open space in the midst of an urban industrial landscape. From the outset, the skills of the clients who would construct the project played a significant role in the design process. We were interested in exploring scales and methods of construction typically beyond the scope of residential construction. As a reult, priorities shifted to the possibilities of volume and scale rather than the complexity or refinement of details.

We began with modeling and drawing analyses of the building form and spaces of the existing site and structure and their relationships to surrounding areas bounded by the central city, freeways, trains, and mountains. Information generated from these analyses of existing conditions was layered with other information to create a complex, yet singular volume to unify separate elements. This complex and translational volume is supported by a wave-like truss system springing from a simple structural frame. This frame bypasses the building shell to bear on six points, four on existing steel crane rails and two on the ground fifty feet below. Structurally, the new volume is completely Independent of the existing shell.

A wall sixty feet high and sixty feet wide protects the translucent kitchen and the interior from the strong southern sun, blocks the noise and dirt of the adjacent train switching yard and forms a protected vertical garden around an existing forty foot tall stand of bamboo. The ground floor is used as a semi-public garden and gallery spaces. A new exterior ground plane was created sixteen feet above grade and is contiguous to an elevated lap pool and to the main living level. Two cylindrical tanks (formerly used for gasoline storage) from the clients' materials yard were modified to make the pool that reflects the downtown skyline and a tower that acts as light monitor, viewing instrument, and hot-air exhaust.

Construction documents were minimal with most of the required information coming from 3-dimensional models. All non-structural steel detailing occurred on site and was determined by the availability of materials and labor. By maintaining a flexible approach to detailing, the project always moved forward. Continuing our previous experiments on smaller projects, "mistakes" were never removed or rebuilt but became the basis for the next set of decisions.

To remember Kathy one need only look at the house.
It is a diagram of her life.

Kathy's genius was evident as soon as she made contact.
We now saw possibilities that were not present
the moment before.

Working together, we transformed how we understood
ourselves and how we understood the world. The house,
as it was being created, in real time, at full scale,
without limiting preconceptions or preconditions, con-
nected us to the world.

We eventually realized that the deeper meaning of
creative work, is to bring people together to dis-
cover their common ground of being.

Whatever flows forth, also remains inside.

project_
date_

carlson-reges house
1992–1996

location_

los angeles, ca

client_

richard carlson & kathy reges

project team_

michael rotondi, clark stevens,
yusuke obuchi, kenneth kim,
brian reiff, craig scott

assistants_

angela hiltz, michael brandes,
peggy bunn, carrie jordan,
james keyhani, gregory kight,
thorsten kraft, qu h. kim,
tracy loeffler, liana sipelis,
caroline spigelski,
james mallock taylor

color + design
consultant_

april greiman

structural
engineer_

peter s. higgins and associates

general
contractor_

richard carlson

The Oak Pass House is located on the crest of a ridge between two deep canyons. The steep canyon walls on the south side of the site precluded building at the brow of the ridge, making it necessary to occupy the top.

We literally reconstructed the ridgeline, keeping the building profile low and mirroring the topography of the existing ridge. Using the surveyor's data points, we followed the site's lines of inflection to create the planes of the house massing. We determined the pitch and slope of each roof plane by extending the visible ridgelines of the highest portions of the site over the lowest portions.

They wanted to re-complete the granite mountain top that was blasted away fifty years ago.

They also wanted a place where they could nest and fly.

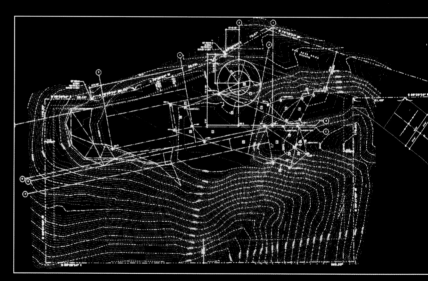

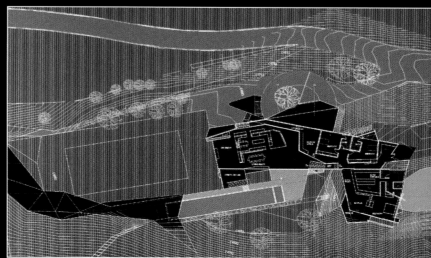

The site's topography consists of an upper ridge and two plateaus that increase in size as the site steps down to the west. The scale and character of the upper ridge and plateau are very different from those of the lower due to a shift in the underlying geology from a horizontal bedded and fractured slate to a more uniform granite bedrock.

The owner's program had a corresponding variation in scale from the largest horizontal element—a tennis court—decreasing in scale to the public zone of the house, with sleeping spaces forming the smallest scale. The elements were fit to the site under the canopy of the roof that forms the new profile of the ridge. The edge of the tennis plane is folded up to contain guest spaces under its southern edge, which also serves to transform it from "tennis court" to "ground plane." The main roof plane dips toward the ground plane, and rises to become tangent to the crest of the upper slate ridge. This roof plan is significantly larger than the interior space it covers, because it was designed to roof the site, rather than the program of the house. This results in a pragmatic outdoor space covered by the free spanning, poured-in-place concrete roof plane. The spaces of the house are arranged around the various planes of the site to create a series of outdoor rooms partially enclosed by elements of the "site roof." Topography of the southeast edge of the ridge is reflected in the fabric canopy that forms a pool cabana on the north and a shade structure at the southern edge of the tennis court. This fabric element links the primary "site roof" plan and mediates the earth and sky.

oak pass

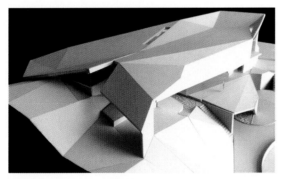

project_ date_	oak pass house 2002
location_	beverly hills, ca
client_	bruce raben
project team_	michael rotondi, clark stevens, michael volk
project assistants_	carrie difiore, nicos katsellis, john pierson, ruhim tejani

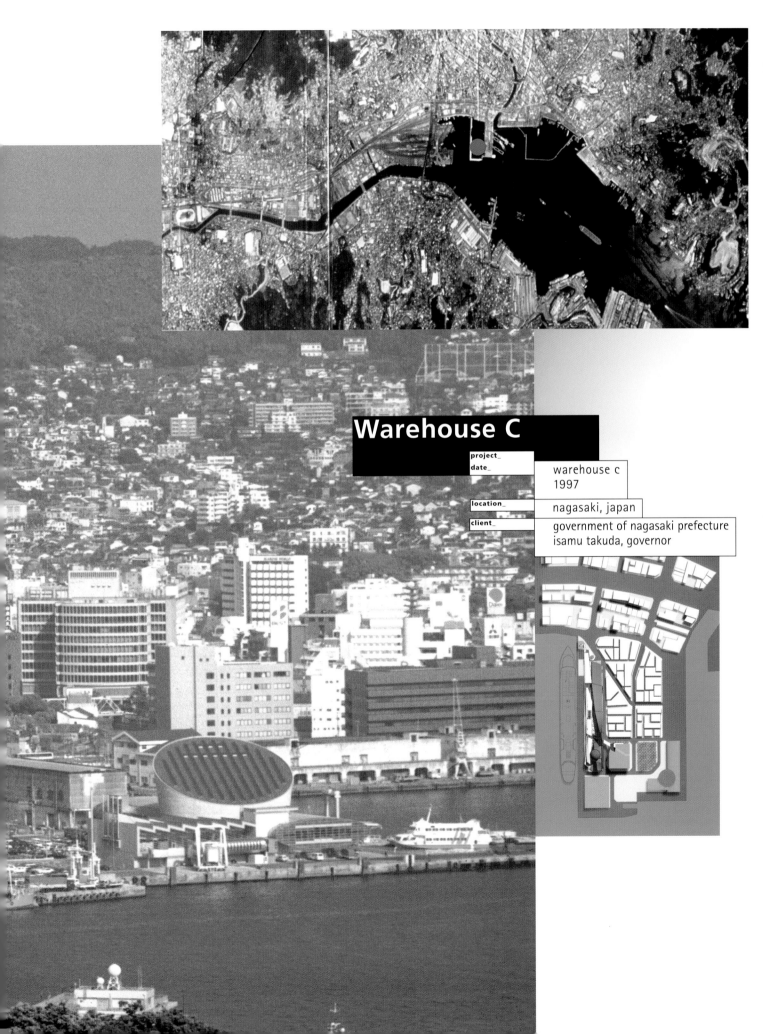

Warehouse C

project_
date_

warehouse c
1997

location_

nagasaki, japan

client_

government of nagasaki prefecture
isamu takuda, governor

 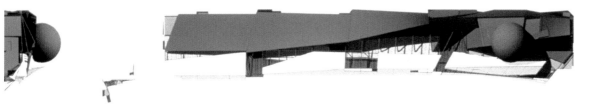 

Warehouse C

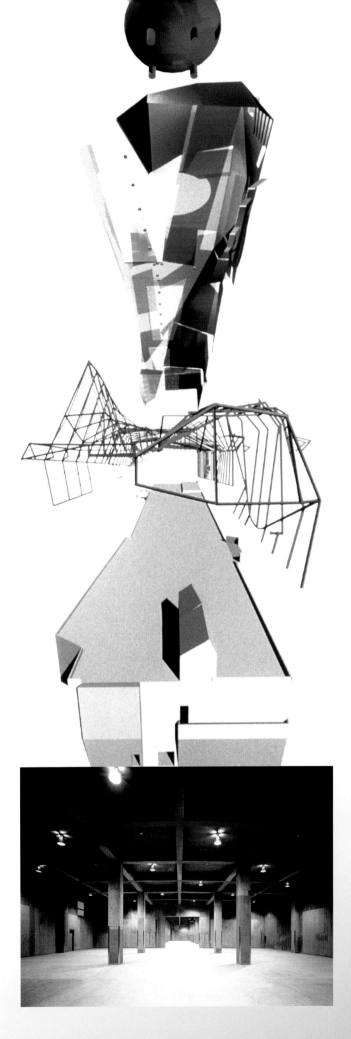

Japan's Nagasaki Prefecture created a new landfill pier, approximately 1,000 feet in length and 400 feet in width that projects into Nagasaki Harbor. The entire pier is mixed-use, with a ferry terminal, large retail structures and working warehouses. The city, outlying mountains and bay surround the site, making it visible from nearly every location around the harbor. Upon entering the harbor, the site can be seen by the passenger ferries, ocean liners and super tankers that link Japan to the world.

Warehouse C is 200 meters long, 25 meters wide and an average of 22 meters high, dimensions comparable to a super tanker. It is organized in three essential parts: a two level private warehouse on the bottom, a public garden on its roof and a 20 meter diameter spherical exhibition hall. The roof scape, a new elevated ground floor plane, provides a public link between the new ferry terminal and retail elements on the new wharf and the center of the city. The garden will be a present day version of the traditional 'dry' gardens of Kyoto.

The overall building is a composite of three construction systems. The base of the warehouse is concrete. The south elevation wall system and half of the roof enclosure are steel plate and the other half of the garden is enclosed with fabric on the north side. The spherical exhibition hall is insulated steel plate, 20 meters in diameter, which is normally used for LNP storage on the huge tanker ships built in Nagasaki.

The steel shields the building from the prevailing winds of the annual monsoons. The steel structure, plate wall, roof systems and the steel sphere were manufactured by shipbuilders across the harbor and brought to the site by barge, and placed by a 60 meter crane.

The rooftop and walls are shaped by a series of non-parallel frames divided into four primary zones. Each zone defines a different type of experience on the rooftop by changing the scale and degree of enclosure of the space. The form that results from the twisting and undulating geometry of the fabric and steel planar systems is a variation on the conventions of the complex planar geometries of shipbuilding.

Seen from the harbor, the building might appear as a ship or evoke the image of a dragon in reference to a significant local festival, or a long lantern.

The Governor described Nagasaki as a place of unity and transformation.
Its meaning and power came from the seven sacred mountains that formed the bay.

It was also a site of memories experienced and synthesized—
first foreigners, shipbuilders, dragon festivals and then the atomic bomb.

Could all of this in some way inform the new building?

warehouse c

project_	warehouse c
date_	1997
location_	nagasaki, japan
client_	government of nagasaki prefecture
	isamu takuda, governor
	hideto horiike, commissioner to the governor
project team_	michael rotondi,
	clark stevens,
	brian reiff
assistants_	max massie, michael reck,
	anthony caldwell, david lazaroff,
	james malloch taylor,
	jeannette licari, james keyhani
color consultant_	april greiman
associate architect_	kiyokazu arai, principal
executive architect_	mitsubishi estate co, ltd
m/e/p engineer_	miura mechanical construction co.
	tsuruyama mechanical construction co.
	touwa mechanical construction co.
	takara electrical, chouei electrical,
	shimazaki electrical, kita electricity,
	mitsubishi electricity co.
general contractor _	mitsubishi heavy industries, ltd.

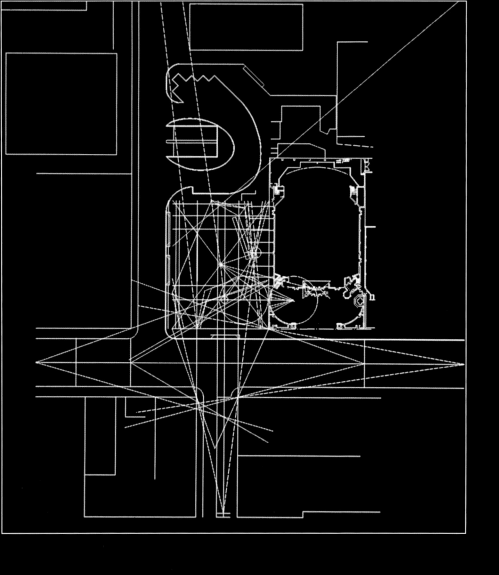

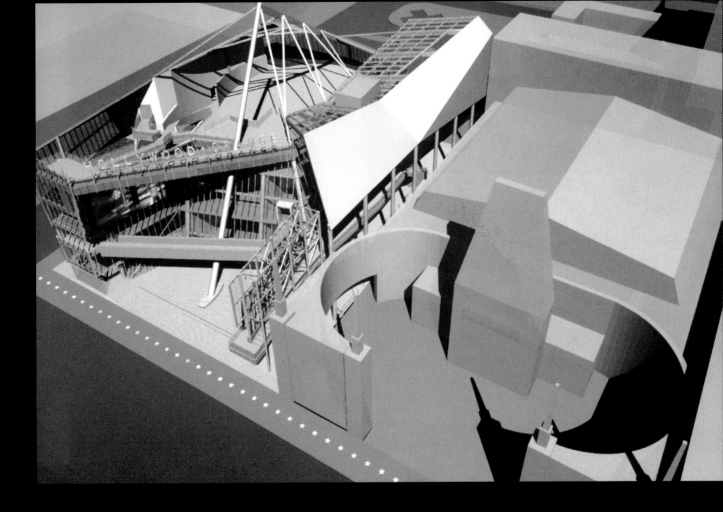

hollywood
orange

project_	hollywood orange building
date_	2001–
location_	hollywood, ca
client_	hollywood orange, llc
	steve ullman + larry worchell

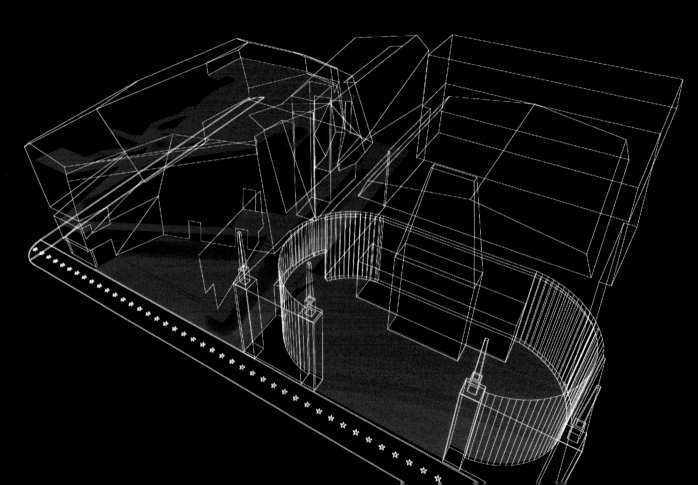

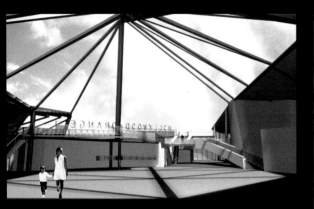

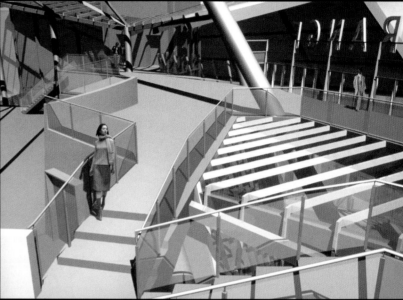

Hollywood Orange

In the past, Hollywood Boulevard was a very social place, filled with crowds strolling, going to the movies theaters, eating in the cafes or shopping. Although much had changed in the intervening years, the boulevard still had the genetic code of being primarily a social space where tourists and city residents came together as they did in great public spaces around the world.

Statistics show that Hollywood attracted tourists for an average of twenty minutes, so our challenge was to lengthen that period to two or three hours. We were asked to make public spaces that would turn the sidewalk into a small plaza, extend the existing courtyard of The Chinese Theater to the west and to connect the arrival court behind the building to these front spaces. These public areas will enhance the tendency to gather and engender the type of resident-tourist community that once existed. We believe the creation of these public gathering spaces will be instrumental in the long-term economic development plans of the B.I.D.

The clients, both of whom have been a part of the Hollywood community for many years, wanted a project that would be a new landmark in Hollywood and understood the difficulty in doing this next to a building of such cultural and architectural significance. Our goal was twofold: to complete the western end of the boulevard where the majority of activity takes place, and to make the space deferential to the existing landmark.

The building was conceived metaphorically as a sort of "anthill" that would encourage people to climb all over it in order to experience this part of the boulevard from the ground, from the second level balcony, bridges and ramps and from the roof deck and catwalk along the front edge of the building. The 1.5 million people expected to be arriving in vans and busses at the rear of the building will be able to walk through the boulevard in a new arcade. The creation of this arcade allows one to move through the building rather than out to the street and around; it also results in doubling the frontage of the building.

People on the rooftop have a view of the mountains that form the northern boundary of Hollywood. From the rear and the front of the arcade, staircases give people access to balconies, ramps and bridges on the second level where they can continue up to the rooftop public plaza. This public plaza will have a restaurant and be used for musical performances or for just hanging out. The building would become an armature for, and embodiment of, public space. In short, this project would pro-

studied our photographs along with various maps. We then diagrammed our own perceptions of spaces in-between, building alignments, building forms, view sheds, proportions and dimensions of surrounding buildings, etc. The form studies were a subtractive process; the vectors projected through the imaginary three-dimensional volume of the site were edited as we modeled the building through multiple iterations, ultimately yielding a final building form that worked.

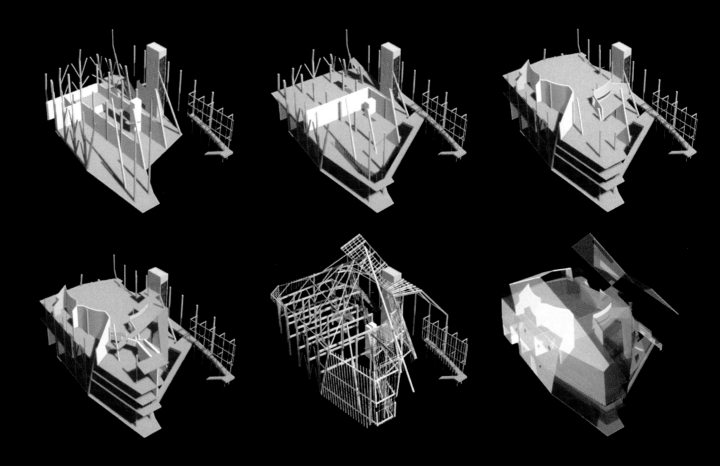

113

project_	
date_	hollywood orange building
	2001–
location_	hollywood, ca
client_	hollywood orange, llc
	steve ullman + larry worchell
architects_	
project team_	roto/jag, joint venture
	<u>roto architects</u>
	michael rotondi, clark stevens,
	brian reiff, natalie magarian,
	dennis lee, dominic van buren,
	giorgios apostolidis,
	nicos katsellis, ben ives,
	jose colombari, jose pablo,
	gonzalez creso, christian rice
	<u>john ash group</u>
	john ash, dick gee
structural engineer_	nabih youssef
civil engineer_	mollenhauer group
electrical engineer_	dalan engineering
m/e/p engineer_	sullivan partnership
general contractor_	c.w. driver

The Elders said to us,
"Listen to our stories and learn about our ways.

Make places for three generations to spend time together.

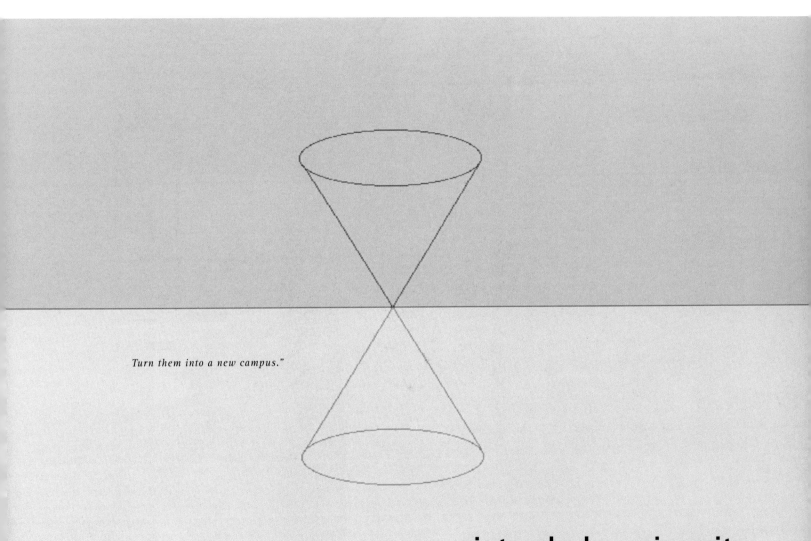

Turn them into a new campus."

sinte gleska university

project_
date_

          sinte gleska university
          1994–1998

location_

          antelope, sd

client_

          sinte gleska university
          lannan foundation

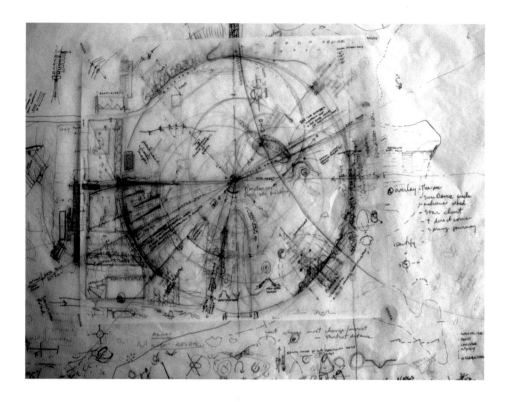

Sinte Gleska University

the oldest tribal university in the Americas, was founded thirty-five years ago by the Sicangu Lakota in Rosebud, South Dakota. RoTo planned an entirely new campus on a prairie adjacent to a lake and built three buildings. The planning, siting and design of the campus was primarily generated by the spatial and formal characteristics of the Lakota universal model (Kapemni) and Lakota numerology. This knowledge, recorded in the memory of elders, is expressed through stories, daily rituals, ceremonial dances, shelter constructions (tipi and yuwipi) and temporary settlements. Our challenge was to find a contemporary form for traditional values and practices.

Historically, the Lakota were migratory people, moving across the plains in accordance with the sun and following the buffalo, the embodiment of the sun on earth. Choosing sites for temporary settlements appropriate for enacting rituals and daily routines had precedence. Permanent settlements had no precedent except as imposed 120 years ago.

The tribal elders believed that it was possible to establish a new precedent. Meeting with them, we learned how they locate their camps, the basis for arranging their tipis, the size and configuration of the encampment and the alignment of built structures with natural ones. The lines of movement and the places of rest on earth are reflected in the sky, ever-changing in a rhythmic and recurring cycle. Lakota myths and legends record the significance of this dynamic relationship of earth and sky, in which the horizon is the zone of human occupation. Their stories embody the concepts of mirroring, scaling, and nesting, all of which incorporate principles of order and systems of relationships between all things in the universe.

Everything is inextricably linked; all sizes and scales, the physical, aesthetic and spiritual aspects.

For example, in the Lakota star knowledge, a system of astronomy and astrology, the configuration of stars known as the animals or the "four-leggeds" and the "two-leggeds" (Tayamni) are stars at the center of the same constellation, as well as their respective prairies in the Black Hills. They are indistinguishable; they are all Tayamni. Generally, the identity and to some extent the definition of a place/person/thing is provisional with regard to context, the relational system that it occupies at any moment.

"The essence of the Lakota star knowledge is embodied in the word 'home.' The Lakota star knowledge tells people they have a place on this earth. The Lakota star constellations, which are mirrored on the land, define and limit their homeland and designate 'here.' The star knowledge also tells the people how to conduct themselves within this homeland. It gives a sacramental and moral basis for the use of their energy, defining what work is and what to work for." (Excerpt from a letter of May 1995 to Michael Rotondi written by Ronald Goldman, a cultural anthropologist and faculty member of the university.)

Traditional Lakotas know all aspects of their landscape, which, for them, have both physical presence and spiritual meaning. Everything in and on it exists in a dynamic balance based on reciprocity and respect. At the beginning of our work, we studied their texts, experienced the land and listened to their stories. We began to see and understand these various aspects of their lives as a unified whole.

We postulated that if the form and physical characteristics of a site suggest connections to oral history, a seasonal event, a significant position of the sun, or

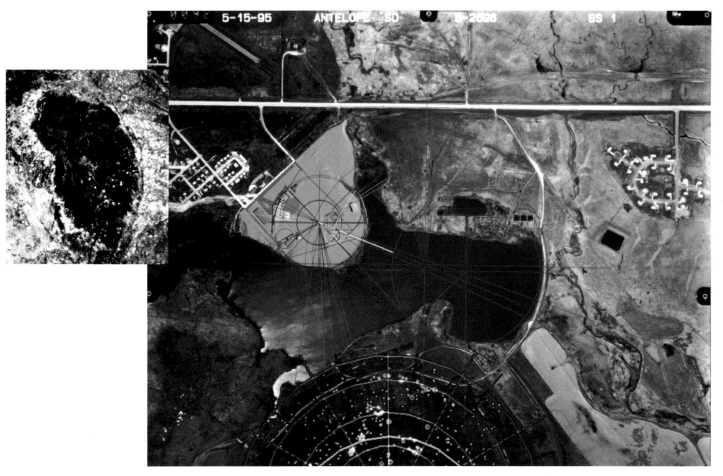

a significant constellation or star, then by learning something about how people might move or where land might be manipulated, we might reflect the traditional Lakota choreography. From the outset, the Campus was seen as an extension of the University's Lakota studies curriculum. We developed a hierarchy for primary siting decisions and diagrams of the campus based upon the number of "connections" or "correspondences" that occurred in a reading of the natural landscape through the Lakota lens.

The campus plan integrates the manmade and natural site conditions dictated by our reading of traditional Lakota spatial systems. We developed relational and multi-scaled ordering systems defined as natural (experience-based), abstract (intellectually-based), and mythological (spiritually-based). Our site began at the scale of the Lakota homeland, defined by the known medicine wheels such as Big Horn in Wyoming, understood to have defined the outer radius of the settlement and its geographical center of the Black Hills (Paha Sapa). We mapped precisely the relationship of our campus circle in Antelope, South Dakota, to all the ceremonial sites in the spring journey, as well as to the paths of the corresponding constellations and sunsets. This process revealed a close relationship, in exact places, between the radial location of the spring

journey sites and the timing of the ceremonies. The Lakota community received this information with great satisfaction, convinced they had made a good choice for the campus site.

The next increment in scale was the volume defined by the horizons visible from the site. Our analysis marked seven buttes to the south, a remarkably straight and directional fold in the landscape formed by the Keya Paha River drainage, with visible horizontal and vertical edges shaped by changes in prairie texture due to shifts in the underlying soil, and so forth. As we pointed these things out to the Lakota, we often heard stories about the landscape features.

Three buildings are presented—two complete and one unbuilt. Their design, construction logic and building materials emerged from our belief that aesthetic issues must be simultaneously practical. We developed these projects as instruments for teaching and learning. The planning and building processes taught methods, techniques and skills of construction to vocational education students, and the construction helped reduce unemployment to some degree.

Our work, which occurred on site (a member of RoTo lived on the reservation for three years), and in L.A, continued for almost five years.

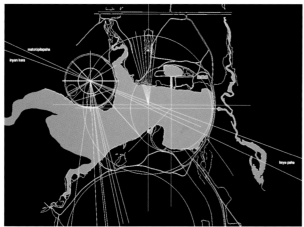

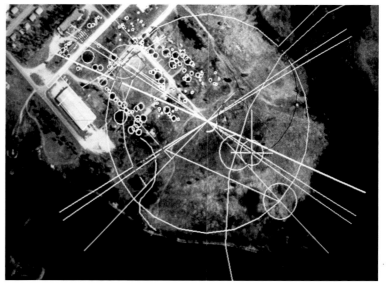

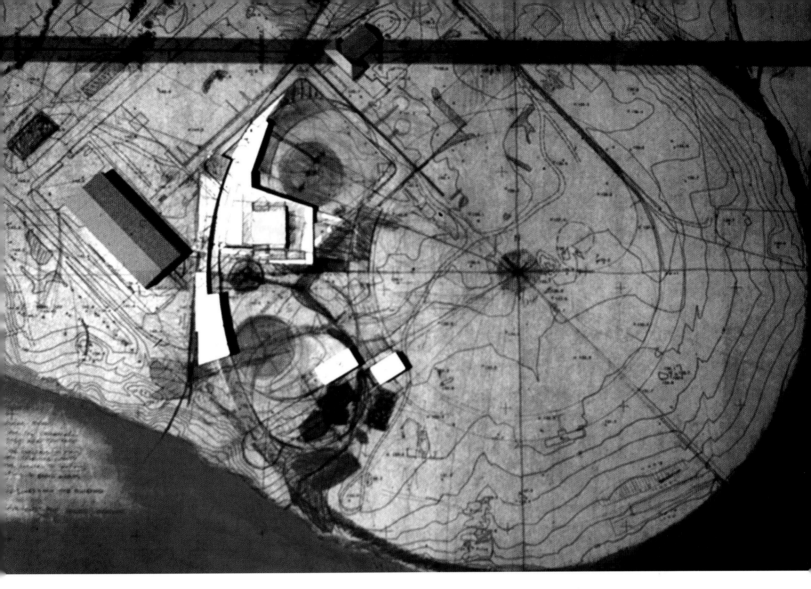

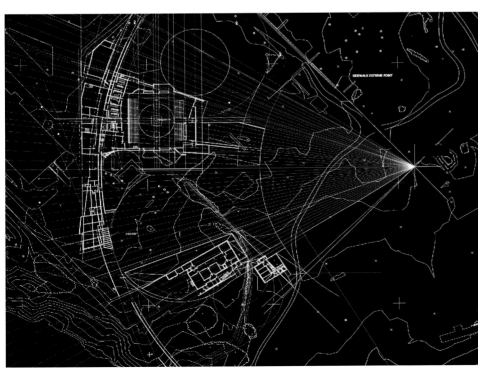

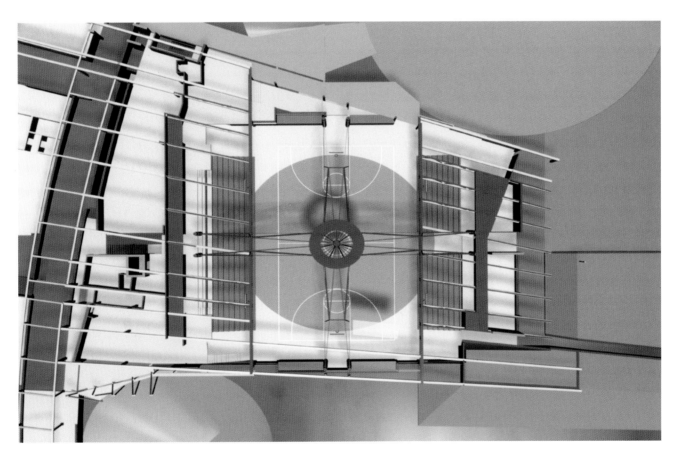

sinte gleska university

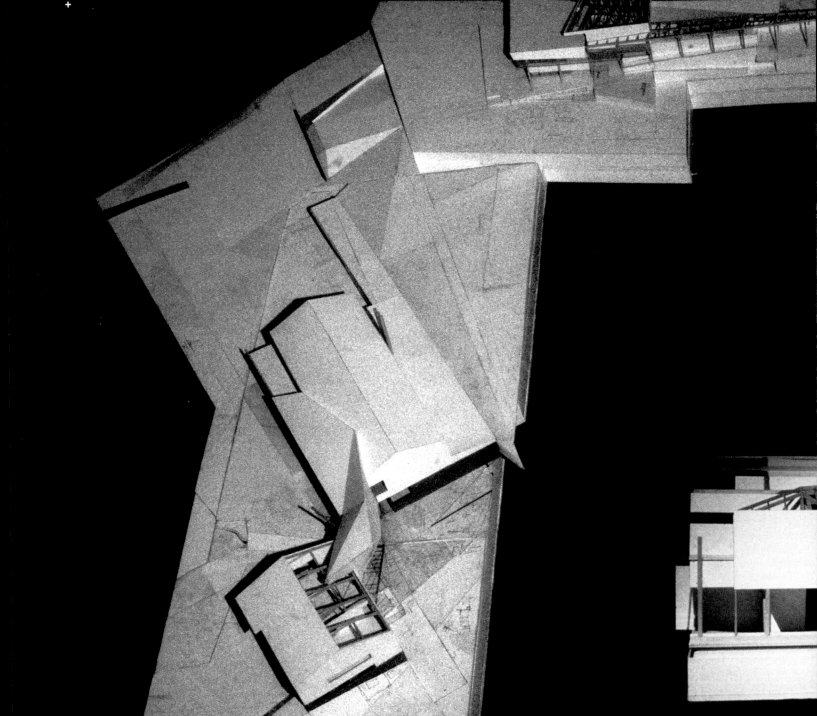

sinte gleska university

project_	
date_	sinte gleska university 1994-1998
location_	antelope, sd
client_	patrick lannan, president, lannan foundation lionel bordeaux, president, sinte gleska university
project team_	michael rotondi, clark stevens, jim bassett, brian reiff, michael volk, kenneth kim, noah bilken, bader kassim, jin kim
project assistants_	carrie difiore, qutt kim, jarkko kettunen, craig stewart, james mallock taylor
project management_	bruce beisman-simmonds
structural, mechanical, + electrical engineer_	ove arup & partners
civil engineer_	dakota railway consultants
color + design consultant_	april greiman
general contractor_	shingobee builders

1994   *"Teaching and learning are among the most fundamental activities of our species and essential to our survival," the elder said to everyone assembled in the hall. Approximately fifty people had come to participate in this informal gathering of elders. They met regularly to tell stories about whatever was of interest that evening. There were seven of them tonight interspersed with everyone else, sitting in a circle just large enough to accommodate everyone. The "hoop" as they referred to it, was continuous with no beginning or end, non-hierarchical and always one thing. It also made it easy to look at everyone there and to look at the speaker. There was so much we wanted and needed to know to do this project. If we paid attention tonight, we would learn a lot.*

We had learned to be better listeners the hard way. Two separate times we were confronted with our impatience. Edna Little Elk was a distinguished elder who had "kept" the sacred pipe for seven medicine men, we were told. She had lived with her family: her husband, a daughter, a son-in-law and two grandchildren. The grandson went on to become the first Lakota to graduate from Yale. Their home was in the remotest part of the reservation. She wanted to live with her traditions beyond the sphere of influence of the "foreign government," and to teach her children at home. After her husband died, they moved closer to others. Her daughter was married to a man who had built them a two-story, single-volume house that employed a sustainable ethos with a zero ecological footprint. It was in a valley near a river and they produced all of their own food. The other families in this narrow valley lived more traditionally. She was the first elder that we met. We were invited to the family house for dinner. She was quiet throughout the dinner and afterwards we all went to sit in the main area near the fireplace. It was a cold night in the Dakotas. After we sat down, she began to talk. When she paused, I asked a question, she answered and I would ask another and another and another until without a word she stood up, turned, walked into another room and closed the door. She did not return, so I asked her daughter if she was alright, and her daughter said, "No, you ask too many questions." I was surprised to hear this. "If I do not ask questions, then how will I get the information I need?" She said, "You do not have to ask an elder questions: first, they will only tell you things that will benefit you; second, they already know why you are here and what you need to know; and, finally, by looking into your eyes they can tell when you have been given enough, for now."

The next time we met, I only asked for her wisdom and discovered over the next two hours that this was truly how we should teach and learn. We met many times after that.

We were pleased to be meeting two brothers, one of whom was ninety-nine years old and the other eighty-nine. They had many stories to tell. As we entered the long path to their house, we saw someone shoveling snow from the walkway up to the porch. From the steady and brisk pace, we suspected it was one of the grandchildren. Instead, it was the elder brother who turned to greet us. He smiled when he saw our surprised expressions. We all entered the house and sat down facing each other. Just as I was about to ask for their wisdom, Grandfather Louis spoke, "I know why you are here. The first time we met two hundred years ago, you did not listen and learn, and we got angry. Now we have a second chance." He was right and we were humbled. We listened for three-and-a-half hours to the stories of the two brothers without asking any questions except for one at the end. "Will you sing a ghost dance song for us?" They did. Once again, this was more than we could have hoped for.

The gathering in the hall began with a prayer sung by one of the elders accompanied by his grandson playing a drum. Together, the overtones of the voice and the beat of the drum filled the space with what felt like an audible version of our own breathing and heartbeat. The figure of the space was defined by the sound. When it stopped, we sat quietly— speaking in silence. For a brief moment, which seemed much longer, it felt as if we were multiple bodies with one mind. One of the elders asked what the story would be tonight. Since everyone knew why we were here (to learn about their world), and what we needed to know (everything), they all turned and looked at us. The architect in each of us (Clark, Jim and me) wanted to hear their version of the story of how they went from the tipi to the box that they lived in now.

Their journey is our journey. The stages and developments in the story are the stages and developments in our lives and everyone's lives; the stories of life nurture us. The darkness of the stories, the parts that scare us, are some of the biggest lessons to be learned. We can gain mastery of ourselves when we are forced into the arenas we avoid.

The Lakota stories are about right relations between one thing and another, and everything else. Reciprocity was the basis of a life in balance, which was the primary objective. Their theory of economy, based on give away (versus acquisition and strategic spending) reinforced their values, defined as co-operation. The actions have consequences, good and bad, in their stories. Lessons were learned in the light and the dark.

The stories begin with fact and expand into fictions that deepen the meaning of real events. They are grounded in actual places, where real and imaginary people and creatures with special powers meet and greet each other. A story can also be a map that provides an insightful look at human nature. A metaphor in some stories can be more than a map; it can be the terrain itself. Metaphor can be useful to model the experience of self-discovery. It provides us with the opportunity to observe the larger patterns, analyze the intricacies of behavior and force us to deal with the obstacles we encounter. We are alive in the story.

One of the Grandfathers spoke. "How did we get from the tipi to the box is a good question to ask tonight. This will be a long story and it will make us remember many things we have been forced to forget. For the young ones here, they will hear many things for the first time, many things their parents and grandparents have never spoken about before. Some of these things will be painful and will make us sad but talking about these things will help us become ourselves once again. This will be a story about our traditions and about how they were temporarily lost. This will be a story about the rise and fall of the Lakota. This will be a story about the nature of dominion.

In asking the question we had naively thought it would lead to a discussion about Native American architecture. The architecture embodied their lives and their culture clearly and thoroughly. It was an authentic expression of their language in the broadest sense. We realized this after the story told that night was completed.

He began by describing the tipi; what it was and what it meant. "It is the embodiment of our entire cosmology and is used to teach the young ones. An elder will sit with children inside the tipi and describe how it is made and what it all means. The practical and the profound are integrated. The process for making the tipi begins with choosing the cottonwoods, their location, the season and the ceremony for cutting them and bringing them to the place where it is assembled for the first time." He described this in precise detail. "The numerical systems were pragmatic and symbolic—the number of poles, their diameter and length were organized three-dimensionally, based on the progression of two spirals, symbolizing two infinities (inner and outer); one descending from the sky and one ascending from the earth, both meeting on the horizon; the line of creation, the domain of all living things. As we made the structure, we told stories. This process served as our work instructions. The structure was covered with a buffalo hide. The buffalo, which gave us food, shelter and clothing, was believed to be the sun on earth, so living in the tipi was living within the sun on the line of creation. Every moment was a sacred moment.

"When the buffalo skin was taken away and replaced with canvas, we began to live in darkness. When the tipi was taken away and replaced with the box, we no longer lived within the sun, on the line of creation. Our entire cosmological system, nested in our daily lives, in the configuration of our encampments, the rituals of song and dance and our social configurations began to disintegrate," he said in a slow voice.

As we looked around it was evident that everyone was sad. No words would ever make a difference. Not long after this we made an architectural study for a fine arts complex that combined two spirals, based on the golden ratio, into one building. It was the tipi and the box embracing.

END

**oglala lakota
fine arts center**

project_
date_
        oglala lakota fine arts center
        1997

location_
        kyle, sd

client_
        hecel oyakapi foundation
        james cromwell, chairman
        oglala lakota college
        tom short bull, president

Oglala Lakota College

We have been working with the Hecel Oyakapi Foundation and Oglala Lakota College since the initial planning and fund development phases of the Fine Arts Building on the Pine Ridge Reservation. The Fine Arts Building at Oglala Lakota College in Pine Ridge, South Dakota, will include classrooms, a library and a black box theatre that will be used for storytelling, performance, filmmaking and fine arts education. It will provide educational and recreational opportunities for the Oglala Lakota tribe.

The scheme is organized into three primary parts: a centralized black box theater that can be opened on two sides—one to the prairie as a backdrop for storytelling and outside-to-inside audience viewing, and on the opposite side, open to the entry "TIPI" used for ceremonial rituals and a sundial. The third part is a long wing for classrooms, workshops and meeting rooms.

The box and the TIPI use the golden ratio, traditionally known to the Lakota as the spiral (employed when building a TIPI). It is used as an ordering system, helping to resolve the unspoken conflict between the TIPI (traditional) and the box (contemporary).

project_
date_

oglala lakota fine arts center
1997 (unbuilt)

location_

kyle, sd

client_

hecel oyakapi foundation
james cromwell, chairman
oglala lakota college
tom short bull, president

project team_

michael rotondi, clarke stevens,
michael volk, brian rieff

color + design
consultant_

april greiman

It was late summer, dusk turning into night. The full moon was edging up over the horizon. The wind had died down. We arrived early, before Earl Swifthawk, a Lakota medicine man, and stood at the edge of the mesa woodlands, overlooking the prairie below. Suddenly, he was standing in our midst.

I did not see or hear him arrive. Jim and I were the only ones surprised, which added to my surprise. We were told by our Lakota friends, all students of Grandfather Earl, that he could move as quietly as an owl flies. Jim and I were the only white men there. We'd been invited to our first Sweat after one year of working on the Rosebud.

In his mid-eighties now, Grandfather Earl Swifthawk was revered among the Lakota for the power of his medicine and politics. He had been one of the spiritual leaders of militant Indians for a couple of generations. He was an irreplaceable "keeper of the knowledge," expert in the Lakota cultural language, and specifically in their system of astronomy and astrology developed over 2000 years. The positions of stars described in the oldest stories verifies this dating.

That night he took us on a journey that began just as dusk darkened into night, one world emerging from another. He had just recovered from a serious illness during which his many friends had all prayed for him and for themselves. This was his first Sweat in six months.

The Lodge was a hemisphere 7 ft. in diameter, 3.5 ft. high, constructed of long, bent twigs woven like a spiraling braid, tied together at the top. At the base, it was belted by a tension twig and the entire structure was covered with layers of thick dark-colored blankets to hold in the heat. There was one way in, through a flap. Inside, in the center, was a "fire" of glowing river-rocks.

The rocks had been "cooking" all afternoon in a 7 ft. diameter pit circumscribed by a mound. I watched Stanley Red Bird carry two orange rocks on a pitchfork from the "cooking fire" to the ceremonial center of the Lodge. These were the last two making a pile of seven. Their heat was intense.

Inside, the ten of us sat quietly, almost shoulder to shoulder, barefoot, clad only in cotton "skirts," facing the fire and Grandfather Earl, who began to sing as he tended the rocks. This was the warm up—literally. The seven rocks, with their orange glow were a mesmerizing sight, and suddenly they disappeared. Where did they go?

The flap had just been closed. No ambient moonlight, and now, sudden darkness. I could still feel the heat of the rocks, but they were now invisible, and I couldn't figure it out.

Though I saw only a blackness like empty space, I felt the presence of ten others. I remembered once reading the counterintuitive words that light itself is always invisible. We see only things, only reflected objects, light reflected on objects.

I remembered reading Apollo astronaut Rusty Schweickart's account of his walk in the emptiness of outer space. When he looked away from the spacecraft, he said, "I saw only the dark depths of deep space and the light of countless stars. The sun's light, although present everywhere, fell on nothing, and so nothing was seen, only darkness."

Inside the lodge, the space was filled with light, yet without an object to reflect it back. Light is always in search of a body to illuminate.

In the hermetically sealed lodge, the heat the rocks put off was periodically and highly intensified by water being poured on them to produce a hiss of steam. The biting surges of heat put us into a trance. Sensing my initial discomfort, Grandfather Earl asked the others jokingly, "Should we cook the white guys?" They laughed. We sang, prayed, confessed, and laughed in a timeless space until it ended at what seemed to be the right moment. I had lost all sense of time.

After the Sweat, we came out of the lodge into moonlight and stood (glistening with sweat) in a circle on the edge of the mound circumscribing the pit, the ten of us leaning into the radiant heat, to offset the heat our bodies were giving off. The air was still but cold. Our upper torso was naked. We still wore only cotton "skirts" and no shoes.

As the sweat dried, we felt the chill night air washing over us. The even texture of the sandstone ground woke up the bottom of my feet.

Our arms hanging at our sides, we slowly and rhythmically sidestepped clockwise, facing in toward the fire, as Grandfather Earl passed on his knowledge through stories and singing. He looked up and read the sky for us. He talked about the inter-relation-ship between sky and earth, how the positions of constellations at certain times of the year were vertically aligned with specific places once part of the Lakota homelands—during the spring journey in particular, three prairies in the Black Hills. The sky and the earth are mirrors of each other.

The clear, perfect disk of the full moon shone overhead, lighting up the sky, the prairie below, the woodland mesa, and a cluster of trees in the middle distance. It was nearly fall and hunting season would soon begin.

Grandfather Earl extended his arm and pointed to the cluster of trees and instructed us to concentrate, not letting our minds wander, on the shadows of those trees. He asked us to count the shadows and then look away. We did.

He told us to look again and count the shadows once more. This time there were three less than at first count. We were puzzled until he told us that the missing shadows would inform the hunters who know where the shadows of the trees are supposed to be.

"The missing shadows are elk," he said. "You must look twice and pay attention to find what you are looking for." He went on, "Hunting is a practical application of 'looking twice.'" The practice is at work in the sacred ceremonies as well as in a reflec-tive everyday life. According to tradition, "looking twice" crosses a threshold, enters into and deepens vertical space/time. It is the deep reading of anything too subtle to make out the first time.

After a brief pause, he continued, "There are many things we normally overlook, sometimes they are 'hiding in plain sight,' and we do not see them until we look again, noticing special characteristics that index an inner life."

My body was still and weightless; my mind clear and translucent, fastening on his words. "Our life is part of a process of emerging, worlds from within worlds—all nested, inter-connected, and continuously transforming in less-than-visible ways." Grandfather Earl described the fundamentally inevitable relationship between inner life and outer form.

He sang in cadences:
A particular tree can be no other way.
A particular landform can be no other way.
A particular glide of a raptor can be no other way.
Sun, land thermals, wind vectors, velocity,
and wingspan come together in that moment.
The glide of that hawk is an index of everything
affecting the conditions of its flight.

It is the same for all of us, I thought.

Earl told us stories until the embers stopped glowing and night began to fade into the faint light of dawn. Just as the stories ended, we looked away for a moment. The moon hung low in the west. We looked again to the spot Earl had been sitting and he was gone. We walked away, silently, the long distance to our cars. To the east, the sky was layered with red, pale blue and deeper blue, light lifting upward. My mind was quiet. The next day, thinking out loud, Jim and I wondered: Can their stories be turned into buildings?

Is it possible to make a building that is less than visible, that can be seen only when you look twice?

END

Joseph asked for a place of

solitude and community

with buildings formed by lines

made with simple gestures.

Quiet buildings with silent spaces

that unfolded out to each unique area of the site.

forest refuge

project_	
date_	forest refuge 1998–2001 (unbuilt)
location_	barre, ma
client_	insight meditation society

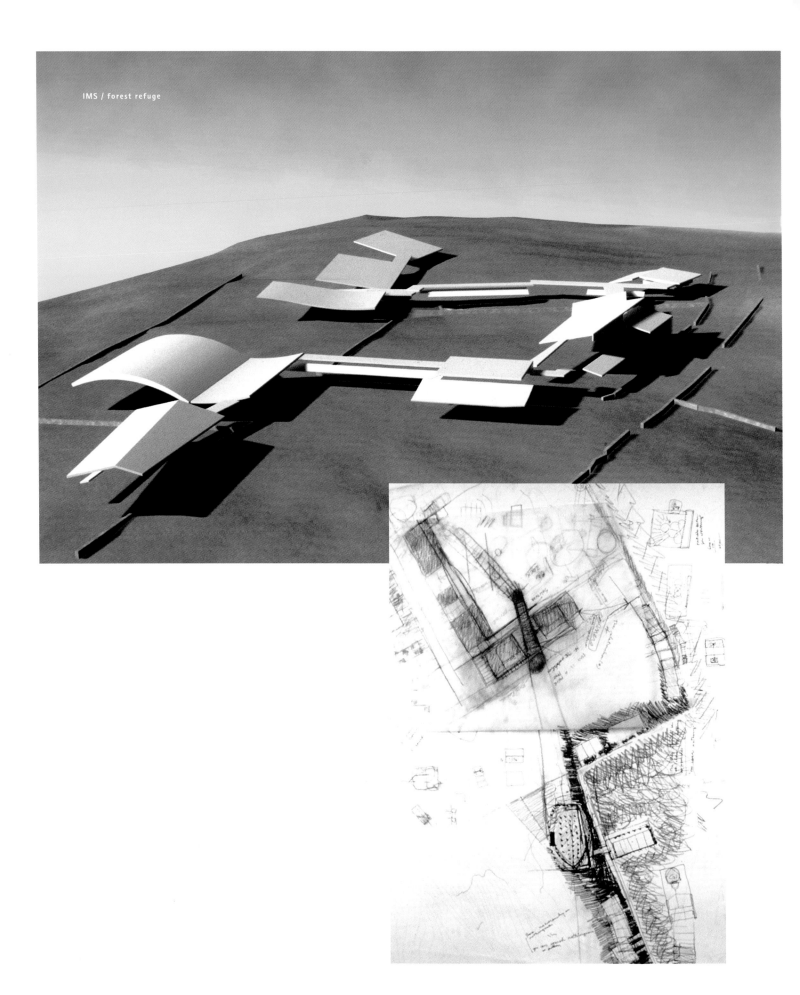

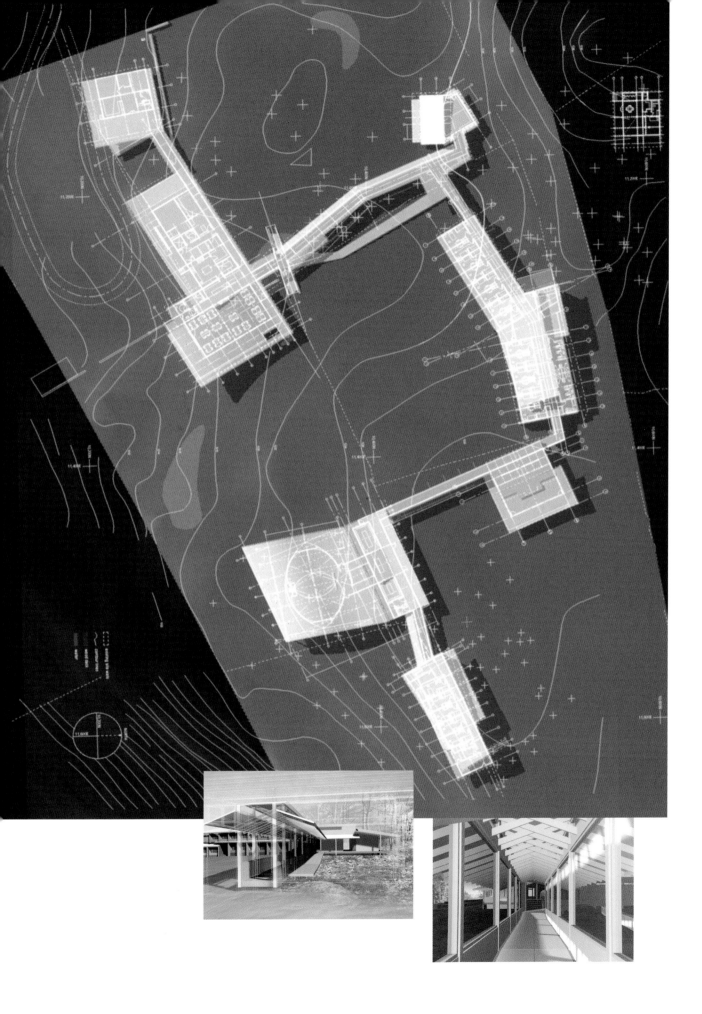

a ceiling like this is
the moment between the
in breath and an
out breath.

is a Buddhist retreat on a forested site in central Massachusetts. It was designed to be a total environment, nature and buildings, for intensive long-term meditation practice. The yogis would have a sustained, continuous practice in silence and solitude, while living in a community of thirty other meditating people.

The seven-acre hilltop site is characterized by meadows circumscribed and separated by trees, rock outcroppings and an extensive field of moss under a canopy of trees; each with its own unique beauty. The entire site changes in dramatic and subtle ways throughout the year. An objective was to leave the site as undisturbed as possible and embed the yogis in these special areas. The three major zones of activity are organized in a linear way, changing direction to follow the line where the forest and meadow meet. The buildings define the spatial threshold in-between forest and meadow. Primary spaces and enclosed walkways open in both directions allowing the yogis to directly experience this.

Nature as an organizing presence gives us a sense of wonder and awe. The integration of the outer world of nature with our inner world creates the deepest dimension of our experience.

The roofs are much larger than the buildings they cover; conceived to mediate the scale shifts between the space of the interior rooms and the space of the site, and to extend the spatial trajectory the extreme distance to the horizon beyond, visible in the fall and winter months.

Retreat participants have their own rooms, designed to allow both sitting and walking meditation for a more secluded practice. The meditation halls and support facilities are all linked by enclosed walkways.

To keep the total experience in a state of elemental simplicity, yet with all of the vitality associated with the spontaneous and instinctive states of perception reached while in higher states of concentration, the architecture was intentionally designed to be "quiet" and "slow." The meditation room in particular is configured in plan and section to embrace (walls) and ground (roof) the inhabitant and to intercept and shape the light to create the sense of being immersed in it.

The brief we were given included the following definitions. Although we were able to absorb the knowledge, we did not fully realize what it meant until we directly experienced silent practice.

Patience
If we have a patient mind, all things will unfold in a natural and organic way.

Silence
Talking distracts our attention. By maintaining silence, the whole range of mental and physical activity will become extremely clear, especially the development of awareness and mindfulness. Verbal silence makes possible a deeper silence of mind.

Bare Attention
This is the foundation of discovery. It requires observing things as they are without evaluating, without expectations. Bare attention is that quality of awareness that keeps us alive in the here and now, grounded in the present moment. The two mental factors primarily responsible for the development of bare attention are concentration (staying steady on the object) and mindfulness (what is happening in the moment).

Spontaneity
When we establish a certain momentum of energy, mindfulness and concentration, we begin to experience only the smooth and rapid flow of all experiences, arising and passing. That is the intrinsic spontaneity of all phenomena.

We worked together, in a transparent way, listening to each other, and speaking only of what was conjured in our minds based on what we had just heard the other say. It was a contemplative dialogue. We were searching for a distilled form-and-space language that would be as unique as Buddhism in America, one that expressed traditional vales and practices in a contemporary way.

project_	
date_	ims forest refuge 1998–2001 (unbuilt)
location_	barre, ma
client_	insight meditation society joseph goldstein and sharon salzberg
project team_	michael rotondi, basil romano, james bassett , claudia montesinos, kirby smith, tenzin thokme, jose gonzalez, ben ives, charles low, jose colombari
landscape architect_	reisen design associates
structural engineer_	le messurier consultants, inc.
civil engineer_	graves engineering
m/e/p engineer_	norian siani engineering, inc.

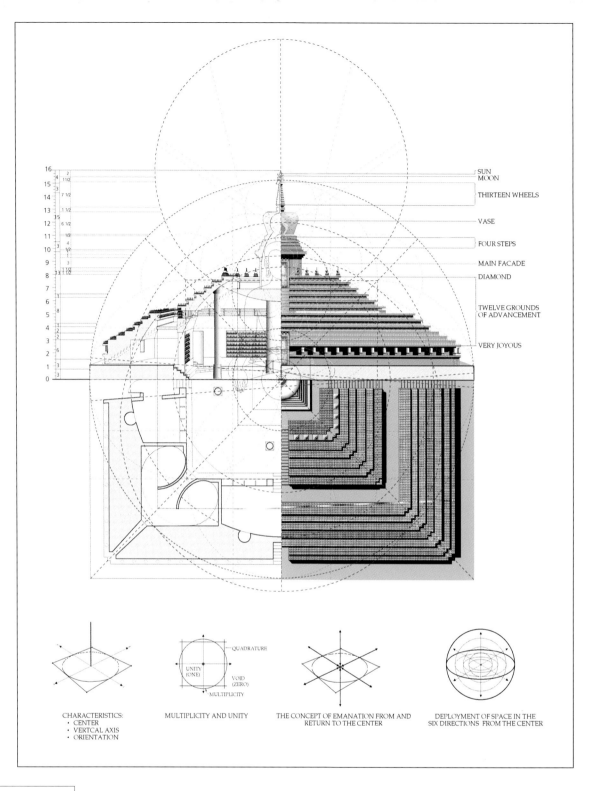

16
4 2
15 11 1/2
  3
14 7 1/2
13 1 1/2
12 15
11 6 1/2
  1/2
10 4
  1/2
9 3
8 13 1/2
  1 1/2
7
6 1
5 8
4 4
  2
3 1
2 6
1 1
0 3

SUN
MOON

THIRTEEN WHEELS

VASE

FOUR STEPS

MAIN FACADE

DIAMOND

TWELVE GROUNDS
OF ADVANCEMENT

VERY JOYOUS

CHARACTERISTICS:
· CENTER
· VERTCAL AXIS
· ORIENTATION

MULTIPLICITY AND UNITY

QUADRATURE
UNITY (ONE)
VOID (ZERO)
MULTIPLICITY

THE CONCEPT OF EMANATION FROM AND
RETURN TO THE CENTER

DEPLOYMENT OF SPACE IN THE
SIX DIRECTIONS FROM THE CENTER

100,000 Stupas

site is nestled in the Santa Cruz Mountains in Central California, at the Land of Medicine Buddha. It is a five-acre hilltop meadow within a larger 400-acre site. The central stupa will be approximately one hundred and eight feet stupa, of approximately 108-ft.-by-108-ft. square and 54-ft. high, will be surrounded by 99,999 stupas of various sizes, placed on a terraced pyramid inspired by Borobudur in Indonesia. The interior space of the pyramid is approximately 6,500 sq. ft. and will house the 24 ft.-tall Maitreya Buddha statue.

A stupa is an important religious monument. It is an architectural representation of the Buddha's awakened mind and represents the entire Buddhist path to enlightenment. This unique religious architecture expresses significant religious symbolism and it is empowered through a consecration ceremony performed by religious masters. Relics and other sacred items are usually placed inside. Buddhists venerate the stupa by prostrating themselves, offering prayers and incense, and clockwise circumambulating the stupa.

The stupa has various forms, however all stupa have certain common characteristics :

1. *Plan develops symmetrically about a central point.*
2. *Volume develops symmetrically about an axis that rises vertically from that central point.*
3. *Every stupa mass is oriented in accordance with the cardinal directions of space.*
4. *The basic geometric shapes are a square, circle and a triangle.*

The structure will be made of concrete and glass, with a wood and steel dome within it. The stupa will be concrete and plaster.

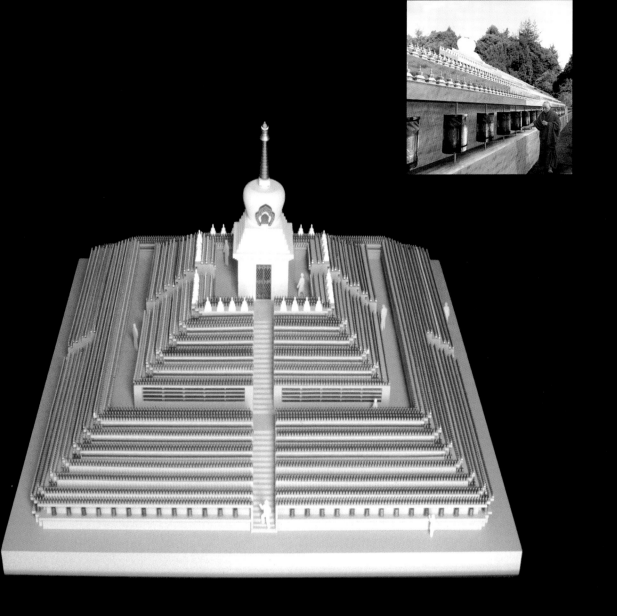

100,000 stupas

project_ **date_**	100,000 stupas 2002–present
location_	soquel, ca
client_	land of medicine buddha lama zopa rinpoche
project team_	michael rotondi, tenzin thokme, tom perkins
assistants_	kirby smith, natalie magarian, raul aguilera
survey_	ward surveying
structural **engineer_**	parker resnick structural engineering
civil engineer_	westfall engineers, inc.
geotechnical_	haro, kasunich & associates, inc.

"A continuous line runs through the center of every solid and void. In a river, this line is where the water flows fastest, with the least amount of resistance—fewer rocks. This is the center line of gravity. If you stay on the line you will remain dry," the guide told us.

We were standing on a wide ledge thirty feet above the first rapids, on the Green River in Utah. Two hours earlier, we had entered the river on rafts and kayaks, beginning a seven-day trip down a deep, narrow canyon carved out by the river. The amount and velocity of water flow was sufficient for rapid down-cutting, creating gorges that varied between 1,000 and 1,500 feet. The river flow alternated between an even, laminar flow that allowed us to see the unusual beauty of the canyon, and turbulent flow, which demanded the highest degree of concentration possible. If your mind wandered, even for a second, you would be out of the flow, literally. It was a fast-paced relationship. You and the river, mediated by a kayak and a long two-sided paddle. As we looked down from the ledge into the turbulent, white water I noticed a tree branch turning over on itself as it was carried downstream. Suddenly it snapped in half and disappeared. I immediately lost my courage and was overcome with fear, yet determined to take this ride. It would be the only way to learn whatever the river was going to teach us. This was the first lesson: the river owns you—you do not own the river. This would be a trip of great humility. To make it through, I would have to strip away any behaviors that might inhibit the spontaneous and sublime play of awareness. Every moment on the water would require my full attention and open-mindedness.

The guide took us back down the path to the river's edge about 200 yards upstream where we had left our boats. The water was glassy and calm there; a great contrast from what we had just witnessed from the overlook. Before I got in the kayak, I looked to the middle of the river and noticed where the sheet of water was beginning to fold in on itself. There was a visible double curling that produced a line, THE LINE. The line is where every thing else is condensed; the eye of the storm. All the power is in the line but the paradox is that this is where there is nothingness and stillness. Then it disappeared in the mild turbulence that was a threshold to the white water. The river was revealing its mysteries to us. I thought of it as an act of generosity, of friendship. The river wanted to play—or was it deceiving us, drawing us in so it could swallow us whole? What an absurd thought.

Leave it all behind. Looking up I saw the gates of Ladore where two 800-foot buttresses mark the beginning of a series of canyons formed by a 71-mile stretch of river. There were no references to scale and the dimensions were massive. The entire region was a part of Dinosaur National Monument; they were the appropriate scale for these volumes. The small thoughts I came with began to evaporate as my courage returned. I looked over at my son, B-Man. We smiled, climbed into our kayaks and moved toward the line. The line would keep us dry.

Each morning the guides would describe in detail the stretch of river we would be on for the day and the best way to maneuver through the rapids. On the morning of the last day, they explained the most difficult stretch. The river was difficult to read because of its changing widths and depths. The surface flow in some areas where it widened was almost flat and appeared slow but below the surface the current was fast and spreading toward a part of the canyon that opened into an immense grotto. In front of it was a whirlpool that was invisible until you were directly on its horizon. This whirlpool was called the black hole. We all knew the story of black holes. If you go in, you don't come out. If you should happen to come out, there is a seven-foot fall to still water. "If you survive it would be a great story," the guide said, as he and the others laughed. The guides insisted we stay clear. B-Man and I requested the only two-person kayak thinking it would be the most memorable way to finish this trip together.

"You take the back, dad. I'll navigate and you can steer," he said as we walked to the kayak.
"Stay on the line," I said. "Remember, use your entire body as one sense to find it."
"May the force be with us," he answered in his usual playful way.

It actually felt a little like going into the unknown, where the most useful tool to get through this would be simple, direct, concentration. Bare Attention.

We were the last ones to enter the water. As we paddled away from the shoreline, heading toward the middle of the river, I reminded B-Man to stay focused, do what he had to do—I would watch him and follow suit. I would respond to him as he responded to the river. We didn't need to speak except in silence. We were practiced at this after so many years.

"We have to be alert and relaxed. We aren't looking for any experience in particular. We simply have to be wide awake to whatever presents itself," I told him. Something he already knew, but I felt it bore repeating.

"Dad, yesterday it seemed that we were old friends, the river and I," he said as he extended his arms and the paddle directly over his head. "It was as if the river remembered me from the day before. It was easy to stay on the line, and enjoy the ride. I was in fifth gear most of the afternoon," he said.

The guide was right; the river's current could not be read with our eyes. We drifted toward the grotto and the black hole. Our paddles were too short to go deep enough to change direction. It would have made little difference—the river "owned us" at this point so we stopped resisting and went with the flow, paying attention to the river. Its shifting surface patterns formed a tense top layer moving in several directions at once. The overlay of patterns read like a moiré. We assumed that the currents below were moving in several directions as well; we could feel them through the bottom of the kayak. It is always a surprise to rediscover how sensitive the human body is in detecting subtleties the eyes are unable to see. For a moment, we were able to feel the layered crosscurrents and make slight adjustments in our direction and speed.

A year prior, we were in Hawaii visiting with Native Hawaiians who had constructed a replica of the canoe that carried the first Polynesians 3,000 nautical miles to the island without maps or instruments. This section of the South Pacific Ocean encompasses the intersection of currents moving at different depths and in different directions. We were told that the navigators had special insights, similar to those of medicine men and priests. They were able to "read" the water's surface patterns and color to determine the depth. They could feel the crosscurrents moving at various depths by lying on the bottom of the canoe and using the stars for positioning. These memories came and went in an instant but were reassuring.

We drifted nearer to the cave while searching for the line in the current that was moving in the opposite direction. Without a word, we put our oars in the water at the same time on the same side, pushed once and the cave was behind us. A moment later, we were pulled forward and suddenly our kayak was spun around 180 degrees and sucked into a vortex of water. It felt like we were going down an immense drain. We had just entered the black hole and were deep in a funnel-shaped volume, a void. Our kayak spanned the space like a beam, perfectly level, suspended, silent, and timeless. We had the extraordinary sense of being in a gateway to another universe. The silence was uncanny. We could see the spiraling current, the smooth texture of the water, the perfect form of the volume that had momentarily seemed like a solid. We were weightless.

As quickly as we entered, we exited. The kayak shot up and out of the hole and spun 360 degrees as we ascended. I noticed the other members of our expedition standing on the river's edge watching in anticipation and disbelief as we landed flat in the still waters on the downside of the falls. We were awestruck as we sat there speechless. We each knew what the other was thinking. I could see from behind that B-Man was smiling as contentedly as I was. We had just been somewhere unexpected and indescribable. We had just made friends with the river. It had revealed some of its mysteries to us. The experience would remain our secret for some time.

With our backs to the shore, I whispered to B-Man "let's paddle in backwards, in synchrony. It seemed like the right thing to do. We slowly moved transversely across the river until we felt the bottom of the kayak meet the sand. What a wonderful sound it was. We were both quiet the remainder of the evening, periodically looking at each other, speaking in silence.

No one commissioned us so we bought a motel with its own hot, soft-water well.

Could it be quiet enough to hear your own heartbeat or at least to quiet the mind?

No thinking, if thinking, think nothing.

We created a periodic retreat for urban dwellers.

miracle manor retreat

project_
date_   miracle manor retreat
                1997–present
location_   desert hot springs, ca
client_
                april greiman & michael rotondi

The first time I floated in naturally hot mineral water and stared up at the stars and constellations,
Was in the desert.

The first time I saw a gust of wind shear a roof membrane entirely off,
Was in the desert.

The first time I saw mountains rising 10,000 feet above sea level,
Was in the desert.

The first time I noticed how small my thoughts were,
Was in the desert.

The first time I sat on a mountain ridge and, while looking to the north,
could see seventy-five miles of valley, and looking to the west,
thirty-five miles, unobstructed,

Was in the desert.

The first time I saw a dammed pond, totally filled with bright green water and small gold fish darting around,
Was in the desert.

The first time the concept of scale shifts, micro and macro, spatial and temporal, became a real-time experience,
Was in the desert.

The first time I watched a meteor shower for hours in the night sky while laying on the ground,
Was in the desert.

The first time I felt smaller than I could imagine, standing outdoors,

Was in the desert.

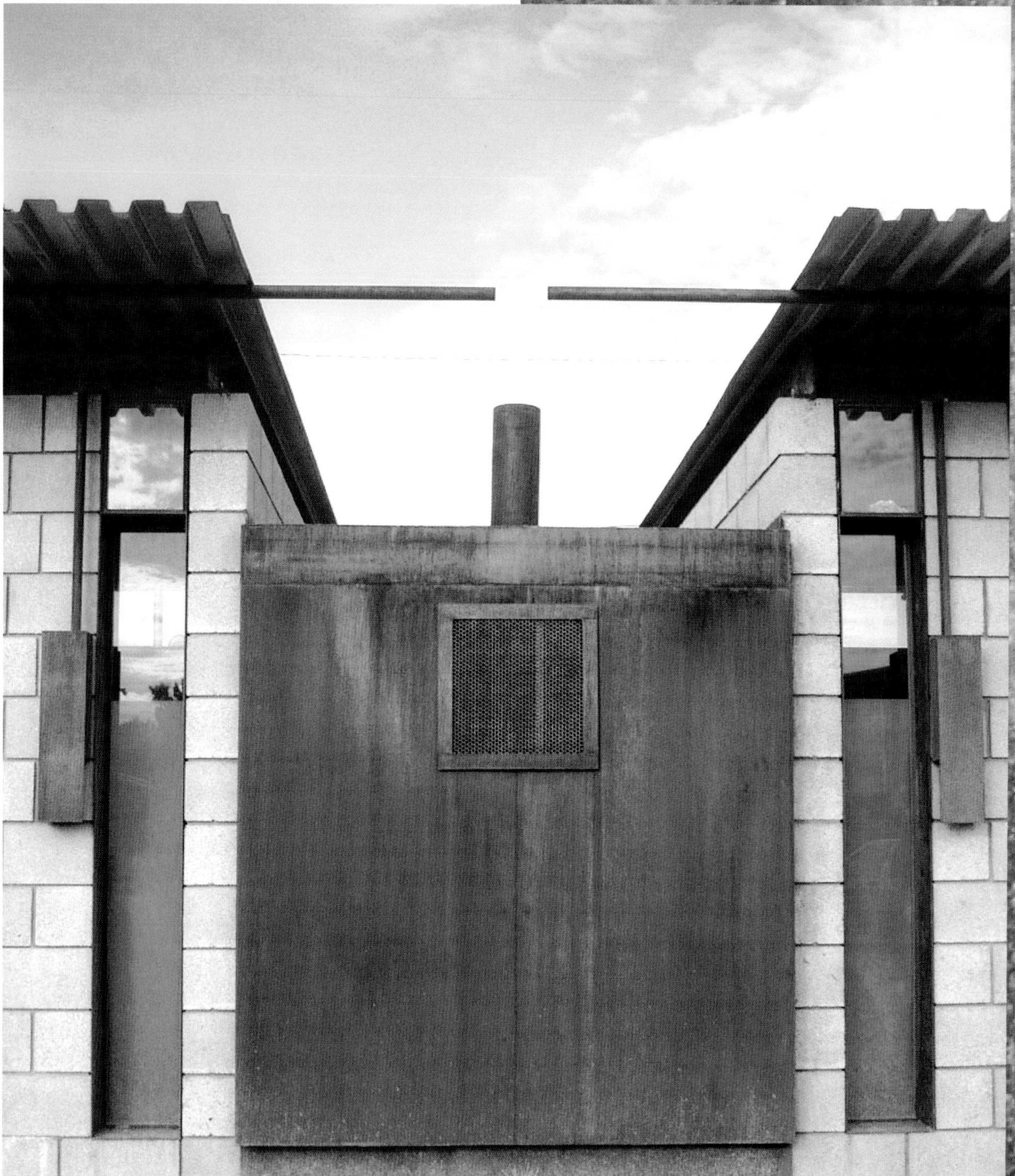

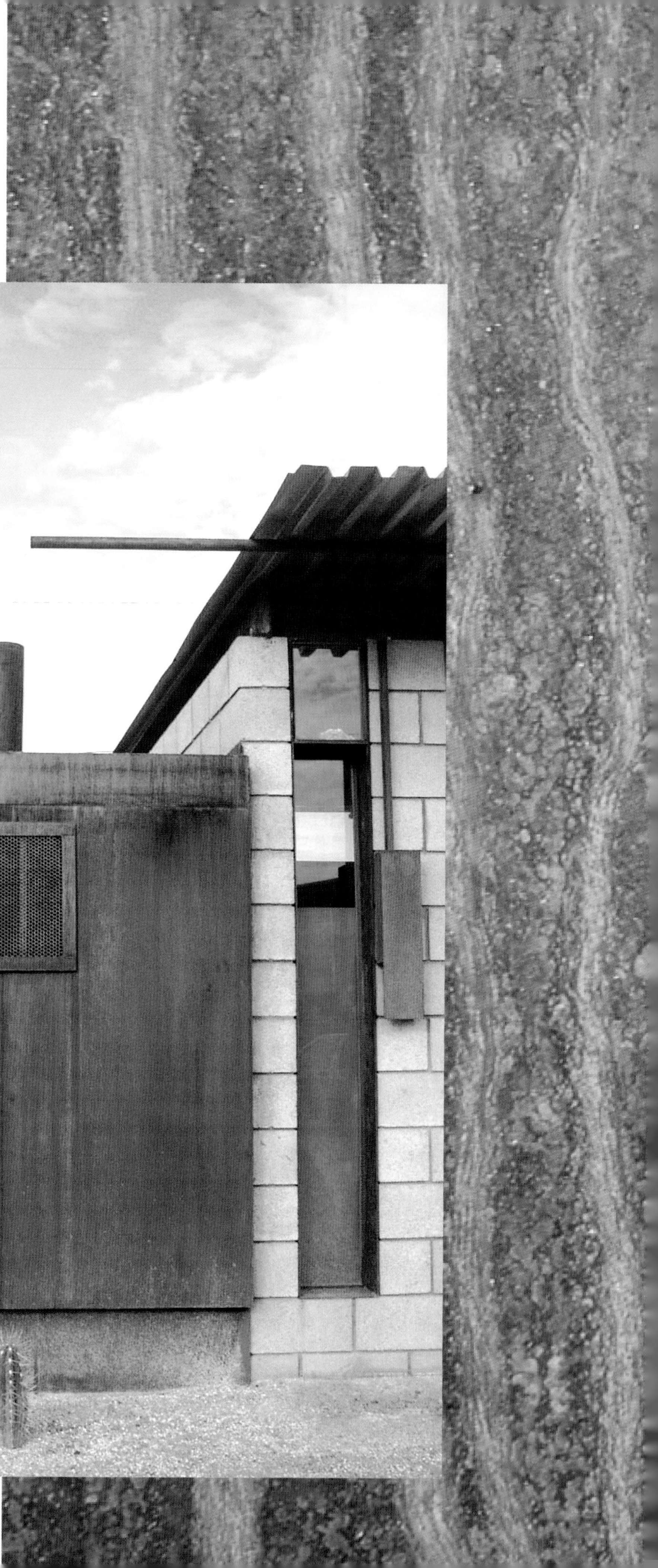

The first time I saw weather forming seventy miles away and witnessed a thunderstorm fifteen minutes later,
Was in the desert.

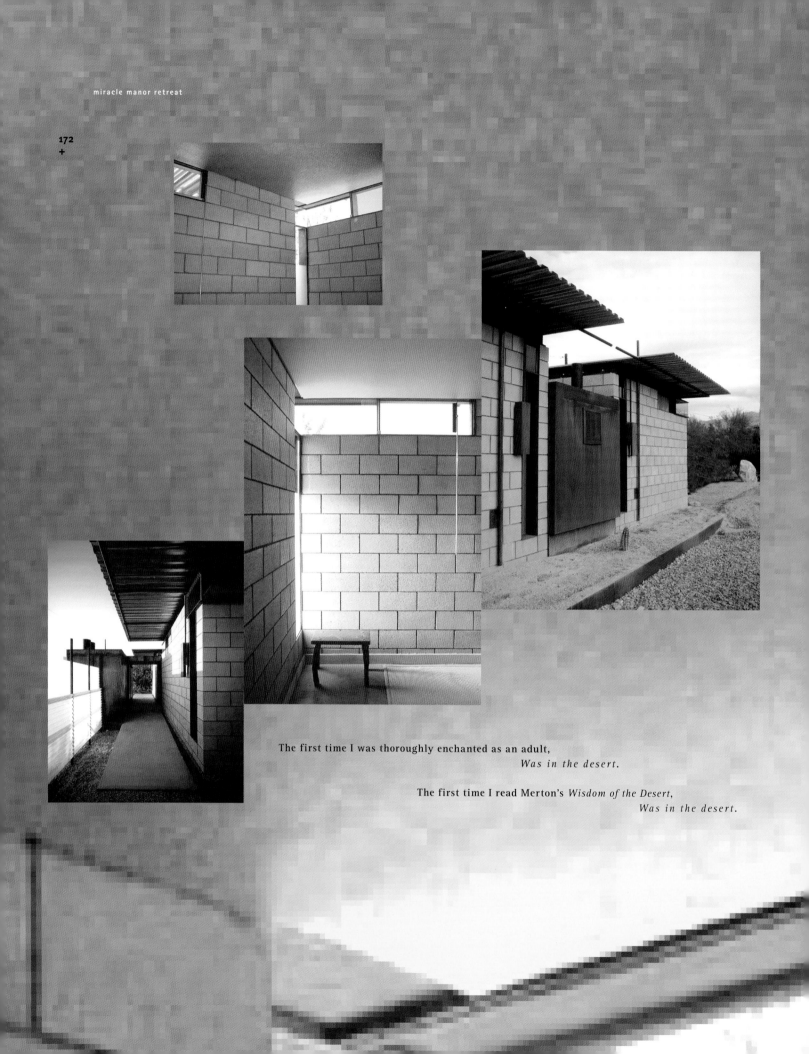

The first time I was thoroughly enchanted as an adult,
Was in the desert.

The first time I read Merton's *Wisdom of the Desert*,
Was in the desert.

Miracle Manor Retreat

Desert Hot Springs is 100 miles (two hours driving time) east of Los Angeles in the Coachella Valley—formed by a convergence of mountain ranges extending from the Pacific Ocean. They redirect the weather fronts south and north keeping the valley humidity low, air quality good and the temperatures warm. The spring snow melts and runs off the mountain slopes percolating to depths of 400 feet where it is held in granite pockets. The subterranean reservoirs are naturally heated to a range of 100° to 200° Fahrenheit. The water directly below Miracle Manor Retreat is 160° Fahrenheit. This water is pumped directly into the spa and swimming pool. Cold springs are fed into the rooms for drinking and cooking.

Palm Springs is at the northern base of Mount San Jacinto, which rises 10,000 feet from the valley floor. Fifteen miles north, on the alluvial of the little San Bernardino Mountains is the town of Desert Hot Springs, where Miracle Manor is located on Miracle Hill. The hill was named for the subterranean pockets of hot and cold aquifers directly below it. The almost flat escarpment was a resting spot for the Indians migrating from the Morongo Valley to the northeast through the Coachella Valley over the San Jacinto range on their way to the Pacific Ocean.

The motel was built in 1948 using post-war construction techniques of wood frame, stucco walls and aluminum windows.

Three long rectangular buildings capped with shed roofs form a courtyard. Originally, the rooms were oriented inward to a garden. Views to the desert were restricted. People came for the climate and the water, not the space and aesthetic of the desert. That changed.

Our objective was to make a retreat in the desert with an environment that encourages a contemplative state of mind. The restoration of the interior of the site, the buildings and the rooms was intended to let the desert pass completely through the site and buildings, enhancing the experience of the landscape, inhabited space, and architecture. The architecture was restored to its original simplicity with a few additions to amplify the desert experience. Design is transparent to experience.

There are six guestrooms with a bed, a desk and two windows, a chair and lights—just enough. There are no telephones, data ports or television.

In front of the site are two treatment rooms—concrete block and plaster cubes with long narrow corner windows—shaped and positioned to spiral clockwise, catching the changing color of light throughout the day.

All of it is done to create silent spaces for being in solitude while in community.

project_	miracle manor retreat
date_	1997–present
location_	desert hot springs, ca
client_	april greiman & michael rotondi
project team_	april greiman, michael rotondi, natalie magarian, forest fulton, adam gerndt, robbie sproull, kirby smith, tenzin thokme, hype-arc, mike nelms, katsumi moroi, steve hegedus, bon & sofia lyman
structural engineer_	parker resnick structural engineering
civil engineer_	mollenhauser group civil engineering

The first time a place was a great teacher for me,
Was in the desert.

joshua tree house

project_	joshua tree
date_	2001–2002
location_	joshua tree, ca
client_	malissa daniels steev beeson
project team_	michael rotondi, forest fulton, adam gerndt, robbie sproull, michael nelms
contractor_	client

Joshua Tree House

_____ is located in Joshua Tree National Monument—one of the most unique landscapes in America. The tree itself seems to be a hybrid of flora and fauna from another planet. The rock formations are large, seemingly without scale, solid mounds of sandstone, fifty to three hundred feet in height and length. Geologic circumstances have made three-dimensional puzzles of them.

Friends purchased one of the original casitas in the area just outside the park entrance. The house is set between two large mounds facing a long view to the west. It had been added onto three times over the years in messy ways. They asked for our ideas about how to proceed. At this time a friend, Sam Mockbee—a professor at Auburn University and the founder of the Rural Studio—called to ask if we could accept three recent graduates from his program. I agreed and we began with this project, to restore the original casita by removing all but one of the additions and adding two metal boxes.

The objectives were :

- to build the most volume with the least amount of surface area,
- to make all of the interior spaces continuous and fluid,
- to frame the special views but not panoramas, to be encouraged to go outside to experience the full scene,
- to use "pure shapes" that would stand in contrast to the surrounding landscape,
- to accept the extreme climate and weathering that results by embracing the aging process and
- to create a house that would be low-maintenance.

The main addition is a "metal box"—a 25-ft.-by-25-ft.-by-25-ft. cube. Adjacent to that is a long, narrow storage building with a roof terrace. The entire interior is "dematerialized" with the use of white plaster.

This project was completed over a period of nine months. Twice monthly we met with the clients and the other interns who were assisting at the site and reviewed the work completed, discuss the next phase and then sat in the shade to have a longer dialogue about architecture. This is a format we use in what we call the teaching practice.

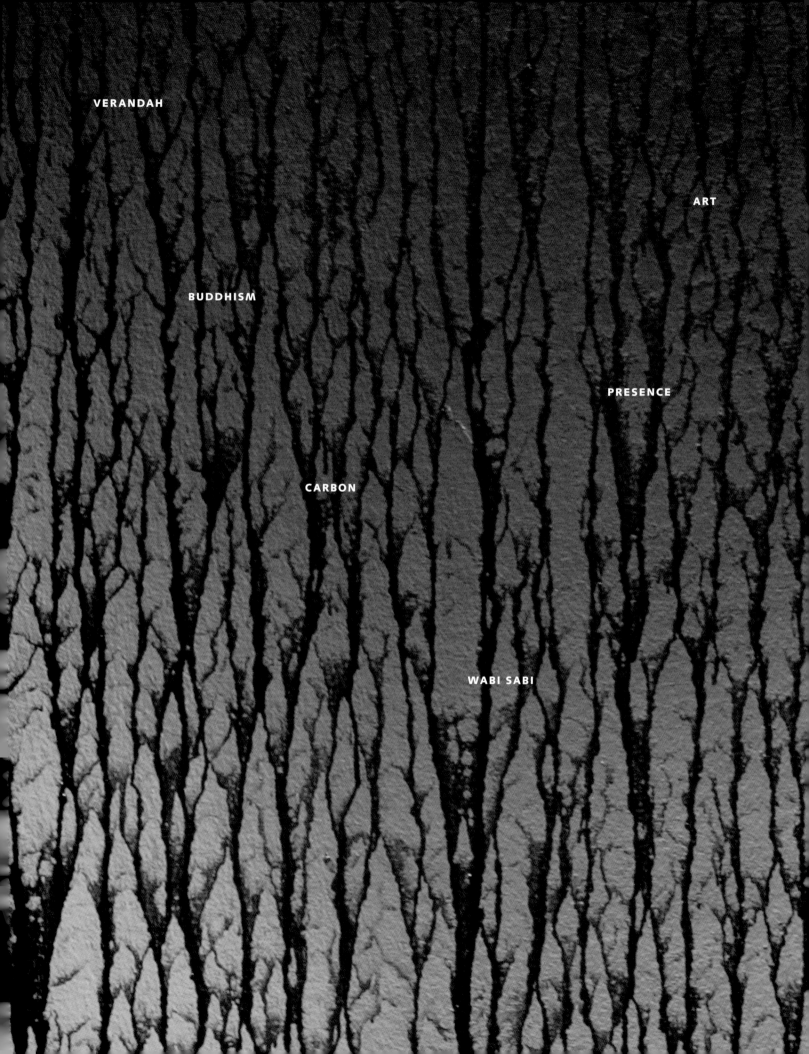

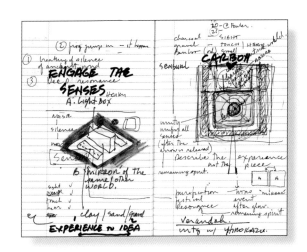

from
the verandah

project_
date_

location_

client_

from the verandah
2004

los angeles, ca

ucla fowler museum
marla berns, director
awake
jacqueline baas
mary jane jacobs
linda duke

From the Verandah is part of the West Coast-based initiative, *"Awake: Art, Buddhism, and the Dimensions of Consciousness,"* which investigates the relationship between Buddhism and the arts in this country.

From the Verandah: Art, Buddhism, Presence is an experimental museum installation developed by a team of artists, an architect and museum professionals to increase awareness of the ways in which Buddhist philosophy can inform Western practices of art production, education, presentation, and reception.

Metaphors and principles derived from both science and the art of tea informed the design and influenced the choice of materials. References to tea, rice and carbon—as echoes of fire, the physical basis for life on earth and the main component of traditional Asian ink—are repeated throughout. For example, all the walls in the entry to the installation space are painted with sumi ink. The central architectural form of the installation suggests Japanese Buddhist temple and rock garden forms, with a verandah-like platform inviting the visitor to linger in a liminal space: between inside and outside, heaven and earth, art and life.

The large wooden verandah is situated within an otherwise dark-ened gallery, slightly raised off the floor, forming two joined mirror-image rectangles. Each verandah half surrounds a sunken "garden." One sunken area displays a marble Rice House by artist Wolfgang Laib; the other, a piece by Hirokazu Kosaka, is covered with a layer of clay that will dry and crack into an intriguing pattern.

A double wall of translucent cloth visually separates or mirrors (depending on the lighting) and defines the two sides of the verandah allowing several lighting options to be employed for performances. Subtle lighting at the base makes the verandah appear to "float" in space.

The space was used for performances by Joe Goode, Hirokazu Kosaka and Oguri, and for teaching and meditation by Yvonne Rand.

186
+

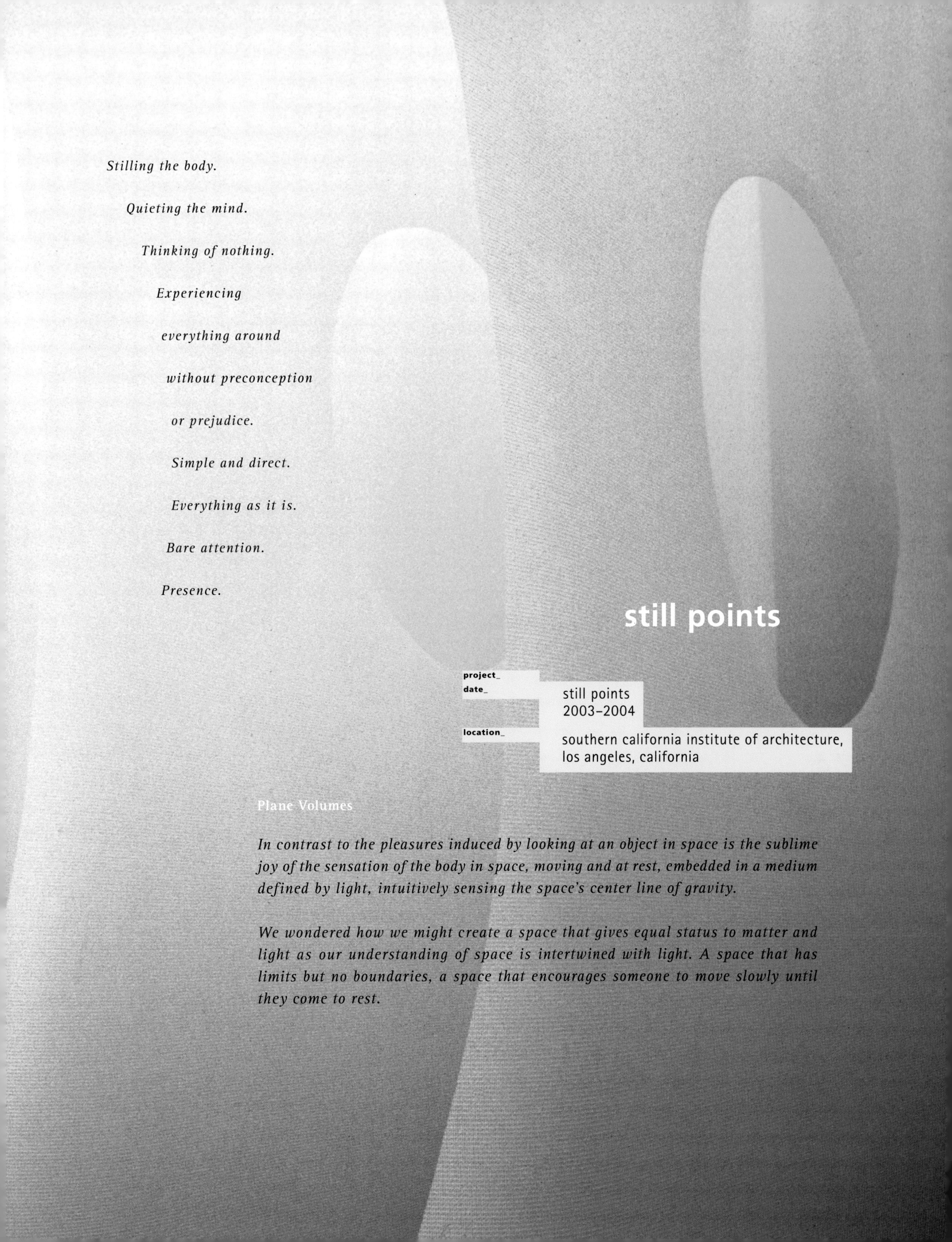

Stilling the body.

Quieting the mind.

Thinking of nothing.

Experiencing

everything around

without preconception

or prejudice.

Simple and direct.

Everything as it is.

Bare attention.

Presence.

still points

project_
date_ still points
2003–2004

location_ southern california institute of architecture,
los angeles, california

Plane Volumes

In contrast to the pleasures induced by looking at an object in space is the sublime joy of the sensation of the body in space, moving and at rest, embedded in a medium defined by light, intuitively sensing the space's center line of gravity.

We wondered how we might create a space that gives equal status to matter and light as our understanding of space is intertwined with light. A space that has limits but no boundaries, a space that encourages someone to move slowly until they come to rest.

still points

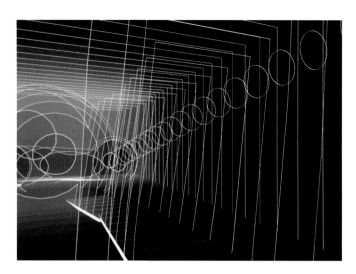

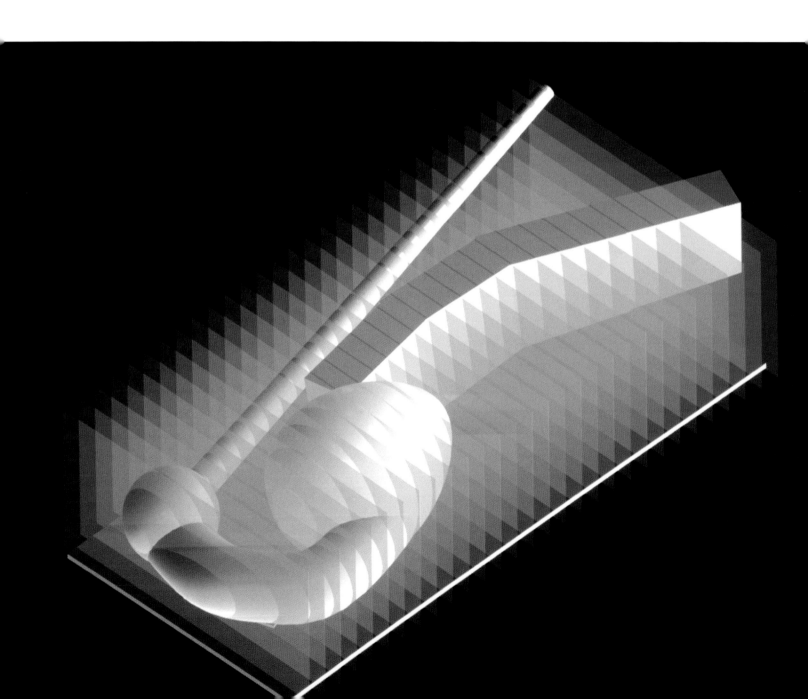

"Who was that masked man?"
The townspeople would always ask.
The reply was always the same.
"I don't know, but the town is much
better now."

As children, we wondered where he
went. We imagined that the Lone Ranger
always returned to a place of calm, of
peace, after his adventures. Alone, in
solitude, was a time to

REcollect
REstore
REcharge
REnew

All that he spent in the world required equal time and effort
to replenish—opposite hand.

He would spend as much time as necessary searching for
the STILL POINT where everything begins, ends and begins
again—an epicenter.

This is no place at all and there is no time.

"No thinking. If thinking, think nothing." He would sit here,
in stillness, in silence, until a feeling of weightlessness came
on. Now he was ready to return to the world and spend it
all again.

The Lone Ranger was a fictional role model. He was generous,
altruistic and preferred to remain anonymous—unusual,
yet inspiring.

Still Points

was an installation at SCI-Arc in the early part of 2004. It consisted of 40 parallel planes of "fabric" 12 ft. high by 25 ft. wide and 14 in. apart. There were three principle objectives: to be an alternative to the solid objects that preoccupy us as architects, to be experienced as both a cave (earth space) and a tent (sky space), entering from the "ground above" down a ladder and into a long "carved" linear space, moving to a larger centralized "egg shaped" room and to represent idea and experience as discrete and equal. From above, the multiple layers that make the spaces are visible, but the experience of the spaces is not known until one enters them.

Most importantly, the installation was to be a place for solitude in the midst of a busy school environment. Solitude and community are equally essential in a creative institution and in society at large. In solitude, we "cry for a vision" and in turn, the insights revealed are brought back into the larger world, simultaneously renewing one and many.

still points

project_ date_	still points 2003-2004
location_	southern california institute of architecture, los angeles, california
project team_	michael rotondi, james bassett, sergio ortiz, kate harvey, kirby smith, jose vargas, john osborne paola zellner, april greiman (color)
assistants_	sci-arc students: eric bono, christian chaudhari, bryan flaig, keith gendel, owen gerst, lorena hong, guy horton, ten hung, catherine johnson, thea massouh, jason mccann, ry morrison, erik schonsett, micah staneley, john walz, yao-hsein wang, alexander webb

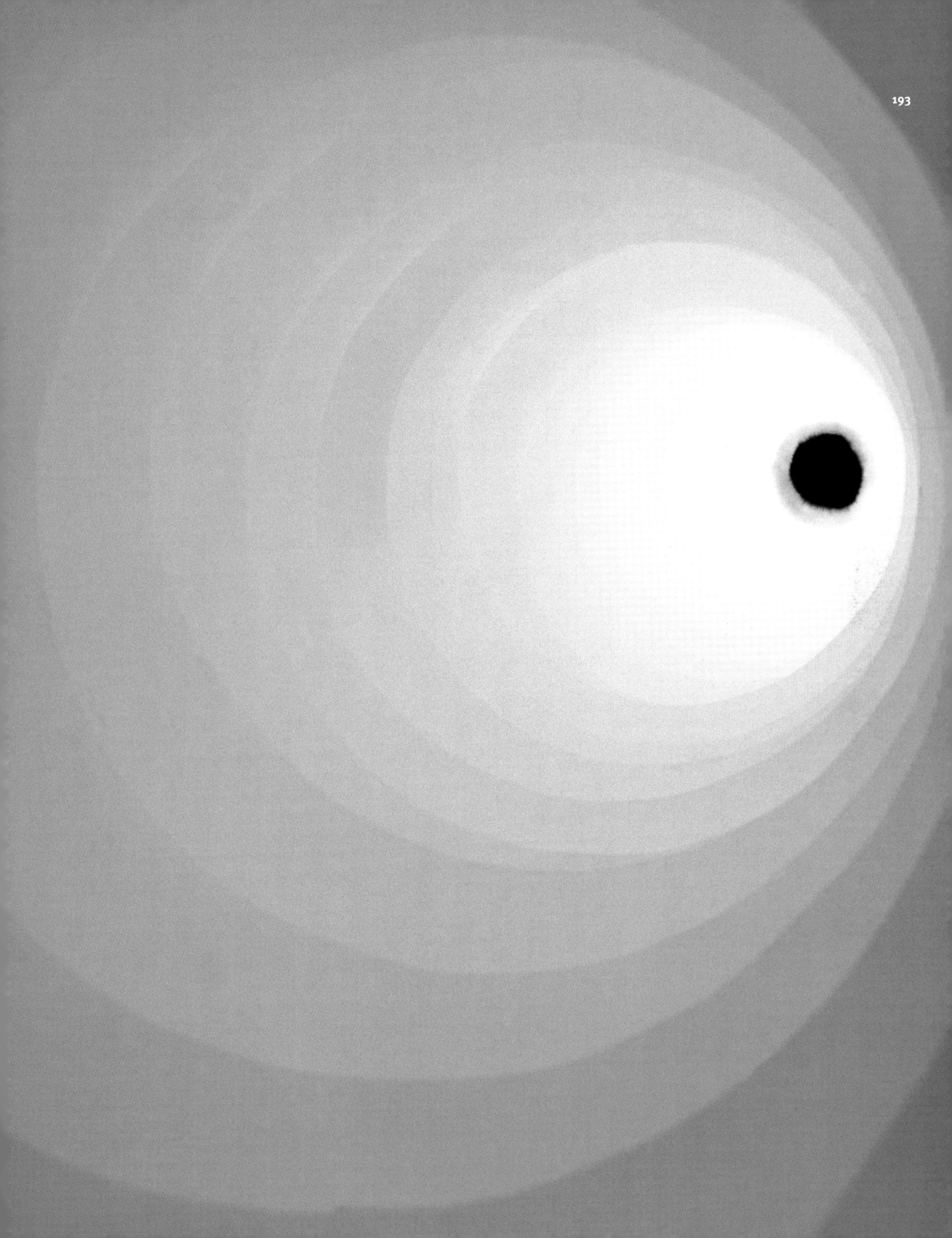

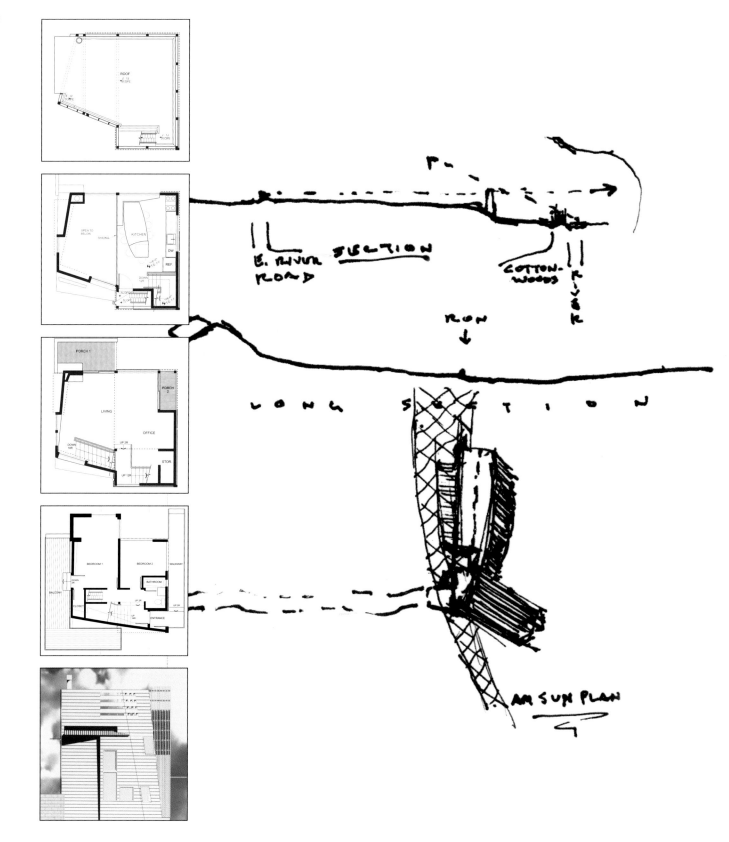

gompertz house

project_ **date_**	gompertz house 1999–2003
location_	livingston, mt
client_	ron gompertz
project team_	clark stevens, ben ives, dave kitazaki, kirby smith, carrie difiore, eric meglassen
structural engineer_	mt structural
structural engineer_	ron gompertz

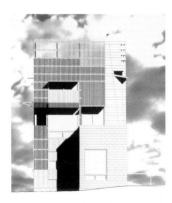
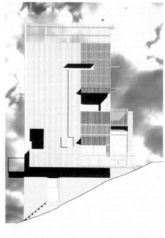
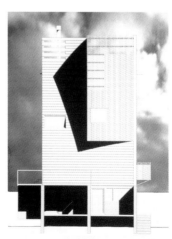
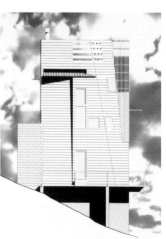

Gompertz House

The Owner's land consists of 14 acres at the edge of the cobbled alluvial fan of the Absoroka Mountains. The house itself sits on the edge of the only sheltering feature in a valley famous for its winds, "Marlboro Country" views, and storms—an ancient bank of the now receded Yellowstone River. The land is treeless, and the perfectly parabolic bank that dissects the property in a north-south line anchors the project. The owner's original program called for a part-time residence to be constructed in two parts—a tower and a hull. The first scheme was defined by a mirroring of the arcing bank, and the creation of a "hull" that hovered just below its crest and opened to the sun and staggering vistas to the east and south. Both phases of that original design were massed low and horizontal.

After reviewing the initial scheme, the owner related the aspects of the place that had compelled him to move back to the valley after a nearly five-year absence—the wind, the sky and its storms. He poetically described the qualitative difference of climbing up to experience the sky, rather than viewing it from the earth. A part of the house, he said, needed to climb above its horizon. A neighboring silo provided his example.

After spending some time searching for a silo that could be reclaimed as a dwelling, we decided to build one instead. Although we would no longer be maintaining the horizontal character of the valley floor, we needed to avoid the status quo massing of the other valley dwellings, which tend to have blocky proportions. Although in some sense, stylishly "contextual," these typical two-story gabled and dormered masses often lack any connection to earth or sky, unless surrounded by shelterbelts of cottonwoods that would not grow on our thinly soiled site. The silhouette of such a typical two-story structure on a broad footprint seemed to block a maximum quantity of sky. We speculated on the character of the region's grain silos and elevators, and mimicked their formal strategy of "axis-mundi," and minimal but dramatic "skyprint."

The View Silo was designed to occupy the smallest practical footprint of earth and the narrowest possible sliver of sky. The building tapers and appears to twist in a form generated by a mirroring of the ancient river bank. Should the hull ever be constructed, it will continue this warping arc in a low horizontally attenuated mass to the south of the silo.

The approximately 1500 sq. ft. program is organized vertically. Entry is at upper grade level, with two levels of sleeping spaces below the crest of the bank, partially embedded in the earth. The work and primary living spaces are located above. A mezzanine for cooking and eating is located within the tapering double-height volume of the silo. Above this space, the stair tower is open to the sky and terminates in a rooftop observatory, the slatted perimeter of which provides a filtered 360-degree view, but tends to guide the eye upward to the sky, which is the subject of this space.

The building is clad on the south and east planar walls by a layered system of 2 by 2 in. cedar slats. These verticals are layered over a water-proofing of brick red asphalt roll roofing. Separated from the surface of the roofing by a 2 in. gap so that all fasteners can be invisible, the spacing between the 2 by 2 in. is typically 1/2 in., but expands to 2 1/2 in. to differentiate areas of the elevations, and to provide varying amounts of surface color and patterns of light and shade to openings behind the continuous surface of slats. When the sun angle is right, these surfaces have the color of a faded, formerly red barn.

In consideration of the initially part-time occupation of the house, to protect its openings from severe storms, and to present the quiet uniform silhouette of the local grain silos, we designed the building's fenestration to be completely shuttered. When open, these shutters provide a variety of sun shading appropriate to the orientation of the facades. When closed, they unify the structure against the backdrop of mountains and sky. Our hope is that at these times of absence, the form will not be seen as an empty house, but rather as a remotely vernacular object that dissipates into and interlocks with the sky.

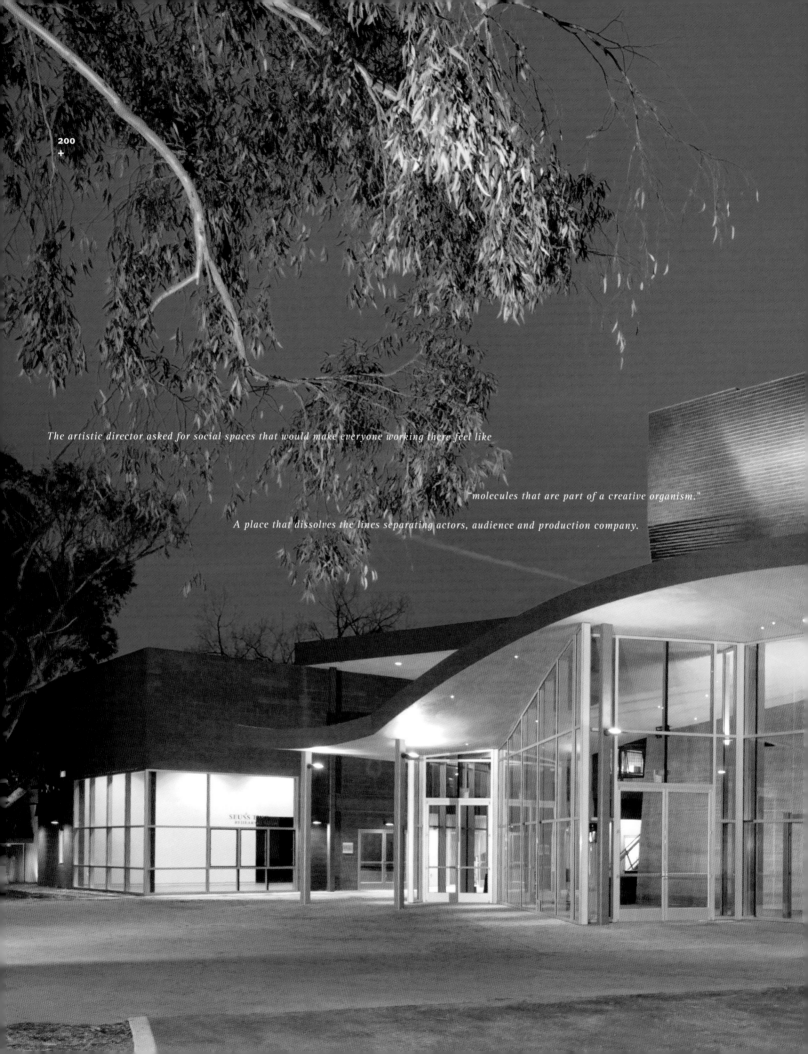

The artistic director asked for social spaces that would make everyone working there feel like

"molecules that are part of a creative organism."

A place that dissolves the lines separating actors, audience and production company.

joan + irwin jacobs center
for la jolla playhouse

project_
date_
location_
client_

joan & irwin jacobs center
for la jolla playhouse
2000–2005
la jolla, ca
la jolla playhouse, ucsd

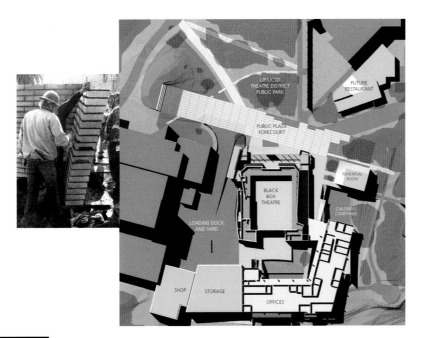

Joan and Irwin Jacobs Center for La Jolla Playhouse

UCSD and the La Jolla Playhouse collaborated to build a Play Development and Education Center located in the Theater District of the campus. The district currently includes the Dance Studio Facility, Mandel Weiss Theater and Mandel Weiss Forum. The project enhances the capabilities of the independent La Jolla Playhouse to develop and stage professional theatrical productions and will support the instructional programs of the UCSD Department of Theater and Dance.

The objective was to create a laboratory for collaboration between artists and educators working on the development and production of innovative interpretations of great classic works to preserve the idea of theater as a large-scale social canvas, which can illuminate and give historical perspective to fundamental American social issues. Another goal was to commission, develop and produce new plays and musicals.

It is a state-of-the-art, flexible, teaching-performance facility that equally supports conventional methods for staging and viewing.

The site planning goals and objectives were to make the Theater District, with its three unrelated building masses set within an incomplete eucalyptus grove, more coherent. First, the grove needed to be re-established to the degree that it could be perceived. Second, the new public areas, walkways and gathering spaces were clearly delineated and strategically placed for ease of movement into the district's "outdoor public rooms" bounded by trees and buildings. These "rooms" serve as the forecourt for the performance spaces. Third, the placement and configuration of the new building helped tie together the site's existing buildings.

We chose masonry for practical and aesthetic reasons. The tradition of corbelling was used in a contemporary way. The lines of stacked masonry were not parallel, creating parabolic surfaces that diminished the parallax problems on the interior while creating an undulating "mask" on the exterior. The integral color matches a composite of natural site materials. The offices and rehearsal rooms with their straight walls are an exposition of the many subtle patterns created by masonry units laid in a variety of ways.

The Play Development and Educational Center for the La Jolla Playhouse and UCSD Department of Theater and Dance consists of a flexible "Black Box" theater, a lab theater, two large classroom/rehearsal spaces, technical support and warehouse spaces, restaurant and café and offices to provide a permanent artistic and administrative home for the Playhouse. This facility will act as an experimental laboratory for artists and educators, and a state-of-the-art, fully flexible teaching and facility venue for ideas and community interface. The urban campus planning goal is to give the entire Theater District a coherent identity and to create a public plaza and restored eucalyptus grove that unifies the three theaters in the district. The project includes 43,000 sf. of building area, 107,000 sf. of landscape, public plaza, and park space with a budget of $15 million.

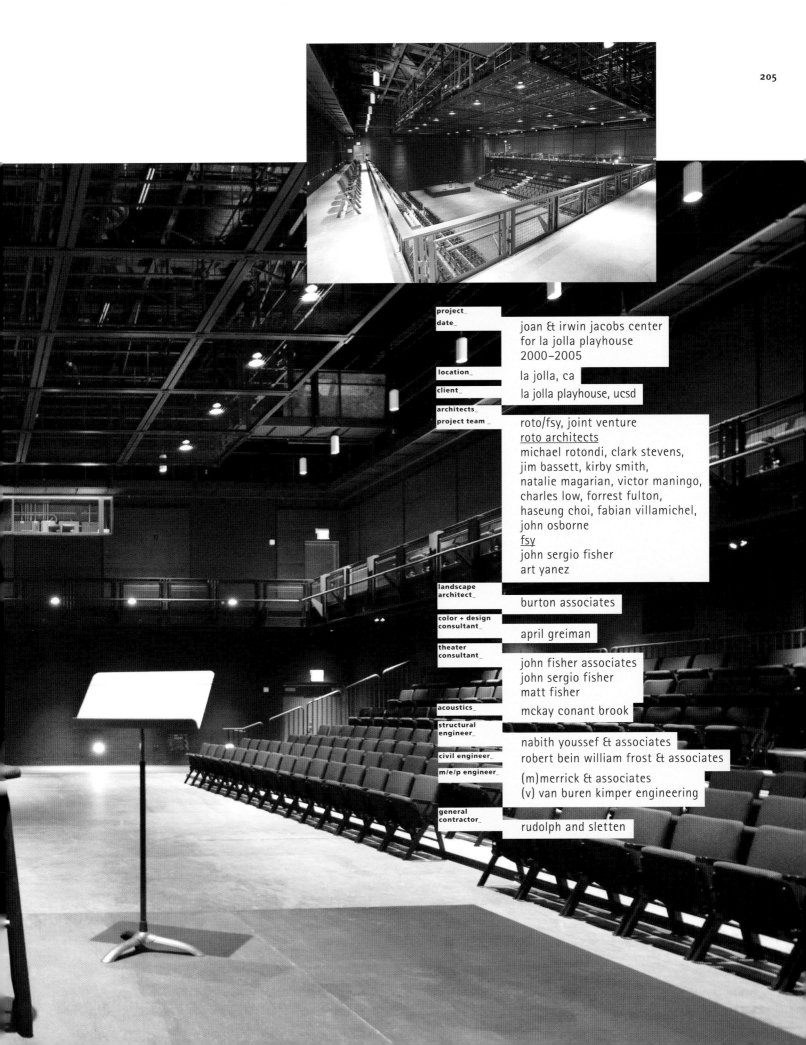

project_ date_	joan & irwin jacobs center for la jolla playhouse 2000–2005
location_	la jolla, ca
client_	la jolla playhouse, ucsd
architects_ project team_	roto/fsy, joint venture roto architects michael rotondi, clark stevens, jim bassett, kirby smith, natalie magarian, victor maningo, charles low, forrest fulton, haseung choi, fabian villamichel, john osborne fsy john sergio fisher art yanez
landscape architect_	burton associates
color + design consultant_	april greiman
theater consultant_	john fisher associates john sergio fisher matt fisher
acoustics_	mckay conant brook
structural engineer_	nabith youssef & associates
civil engineer_	robert bein william frost & associates
m/e/p engineer_	(m) merrick & associates (v) van buren kimper engineering
general contractor_	rudolph and sletten

prairie view
a + m university
architecture +
art building

project_
date_
    prairie view a&m university
    architecture and art building
    2003–2005

location_
    prairie view, tx

client_
    texas a&m university system
    pvamu, dr. ikhlas sabouni, dean

an architecture school should
embody the universal and the particular intelligence

beginning with gravity and light.

The process of making and building

learning and teaching.

Context and

hypertext might become operative terms

The president of the school said an architecture school should
embody the universal and the particular intelligence about
all aspects of the world, beginning with gravity and light.
The process of making and building itself
can be instrumental in learning and teaching.
Context and hypertext might become operative terms.

out

yend

flow thru →

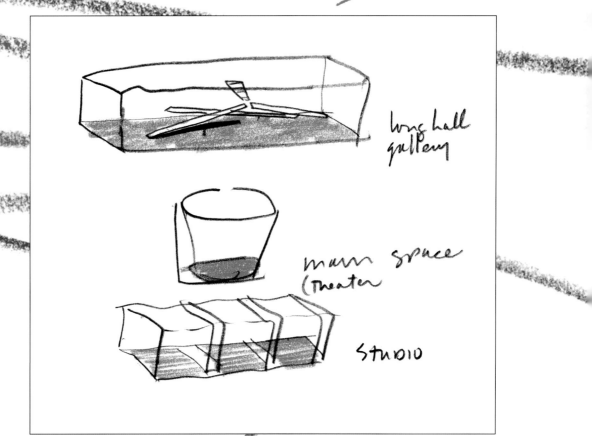

long hall gallery

main space (theater

studio

he Canyons,

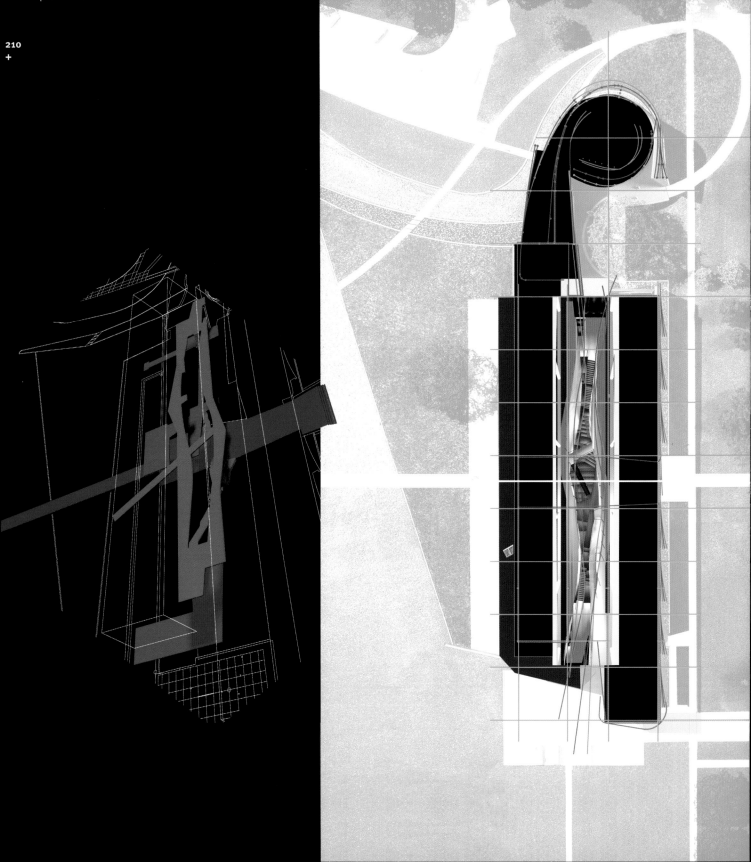

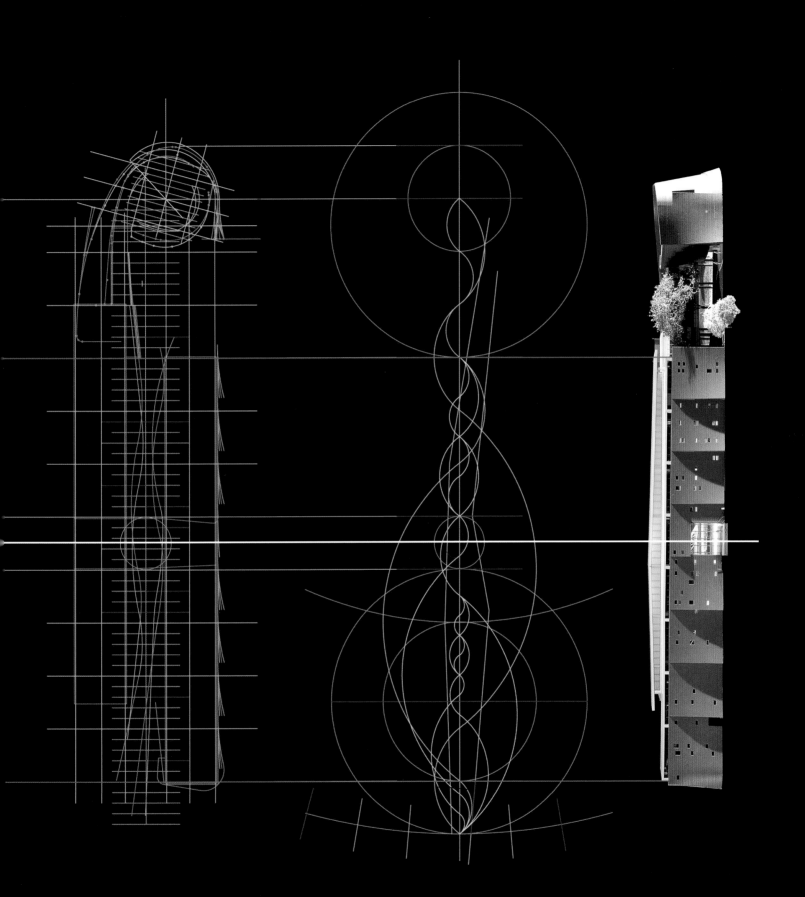

The site is a gateway to the campus. Located on a corner site at the main entrance to the campus, the project is connected to the rest of the campus by a pedestrian street running east to west across the campus. The Art and Architecture Building is located on the east end of the mall and a recently completed student center is located at the west end. The campus is to the north of the building and a prairie is to the south.

Several significant oak trees line the entry to the campus and the pedestrian mall and are scattered across the site forming a natural tree circle to the south. One of the oldest and largest trees, a 100-year-old oak with a 70 ft. diameter, is the focus of the entry court between the new Cultural Center and Art and Architecture buildings. Native prairie grass is the dominant ground cover.

This public university is the second oldest institution of higher education in Texas, founded 106 years ago and the first in that state to be devoted to equal education for African Americans. The architecture program was founded forty years ago and was a part of the College of Engineering. Recently, it has become its own college.

The new 110,000 sq. ft. building includes the architecture program, the art program, Construction Sciences, the CURES Center (Center for Community Urban and Rural Extension Services) and the Cultural Center.

The project is situated on its site with permeable boundaries ready to accept any of the vectors of people coming from different locations. The Cultural Center, the circulatory vortex at the front, is the social memory and genesis of the primary ordering lines that move the length of the site, shaping the volumes. The incremental and linear system interprets the musical structures of traditional African music at the core of contemporary music.

The formal teaching spaces are in long bars distributed over three floors. These two rectangles create an in-between space—the canyon—the main social space where all the public activities take place and are visible from any place on any level. This exchange zone is the site of intense informal learning and teaching and where everyone directly experiences their common ground of being.

The building is organized in two parts: the head and the body. The head, the Cultural Center, is for archiving and exhibiting African-American history in central Texas. Conceptually this is the memory of the people who settled this land and created this historic school.

Knowledge resides here.

The body is the creative laboratory.

Practice resides here.

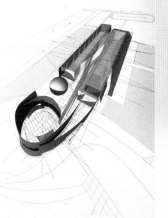

The design studios and workshops are on the first and third floors of this three-story building. They sandwich classrooms and offices in between.

Lines spiral out from the epicenter of the Cultural Center in rhythmic waves marked periodically by incremental crosscurrent lines. A composite musical notation drawing was constructed by sampling African American music for the purpose of embedding it in the initial diagram.

The central volume of this long, rectilinear prism is "eroded" throughout, into a canyon-like space, which expands and contracts according to the type and intensity of uses. There is a conceptual centerline of gravity that extends the entire length. The "canyon" is the social space of the school, used for teaching, presentations, and hanging out.

As the lines flow through this zone, there is an intensification of the flow—a turbulence or vortex—at the midpoint. This is the main gathering space of the school. Here is where a contemporary interpretation of Rome's Spanish Steps begin their ascent. This fluid interior space creates numerous places for social exchange and dialogue that are critical to the development of an educational community focused on encouraging cooperation rather than competition.

The experience of the building's rhythms is intended to regulate your speed until you begin to move more deliberately and slowly, with periodic pauses, to view up, down, across, or through, vicariously participating in everything happening.

The mandate to make a brick building was an opportunity to explore this ancient craft. Unit and multiple, scale shifting, weight, and plasticity were conceptual frames of reference. Curvilinear corbeling was the basic technique used to make the walls. On the north façade, the brick peels away like curtains to allow slots of light into the classrooms and center of the building.

These curtains are cantilevered and float above the ground. The brick Cultural Center is linked to the rest of the building through a structural module and proportioning system thus remaining an identifiable element but also a part of the whole.

Meeting with faculty and students, we discussed ways in which this project could be a vehicle for teaching, and for developing a deeper understanding of the creative process for architects, which is individually formed and communally realized. We met with the students and faculty throughout the design and construction process, in lecture and seminar format, to discuss various aspects of the project, and to learn. The primary objective has been to create the conditions that would en courage people to do their best work.

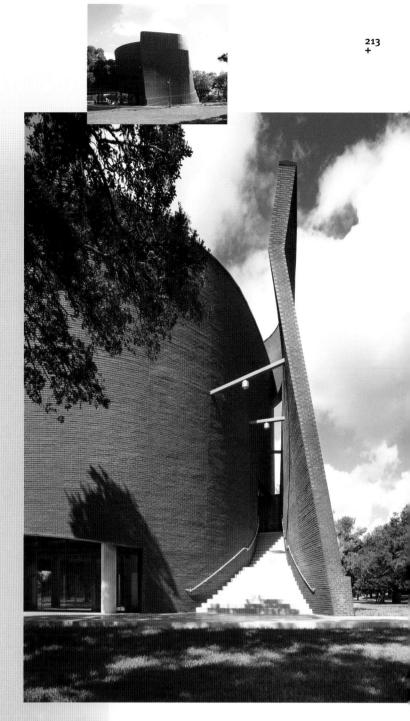

prairie view

campus

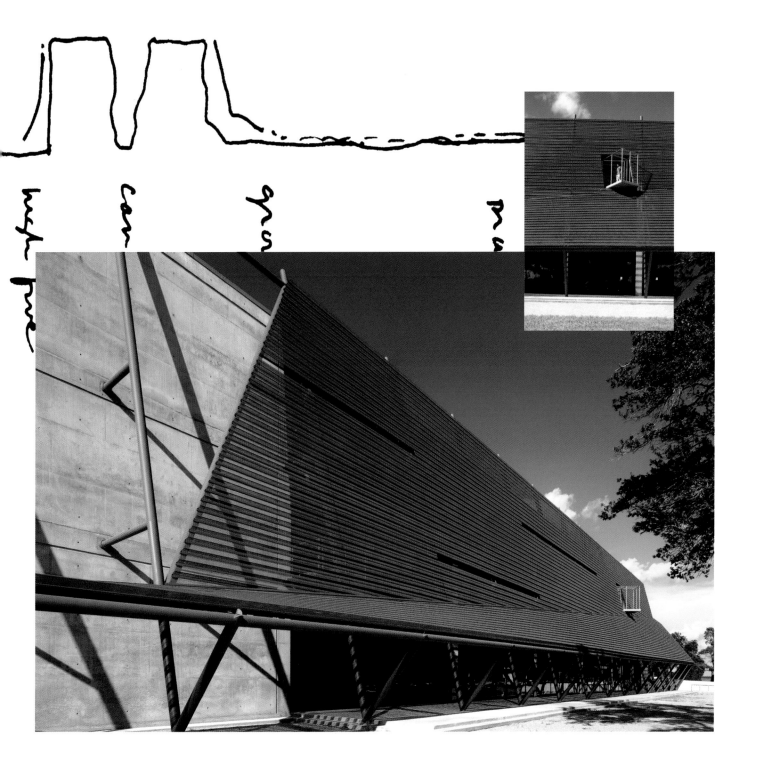

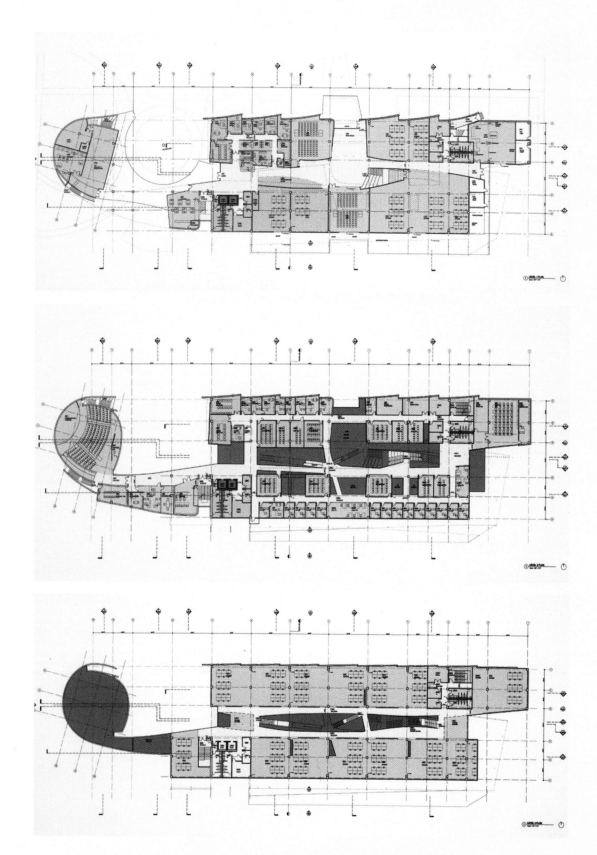

project_ **date_**	prairie view a&m university architecture and art building 2003–2005
location_	prairie view, tx
client_	texas a&m university system pvamu, dr. ikhlas sabouni, dean
architects_ **project team_**	roto/hks, joint venture <u>roto architects</u> michael rotondi, clark stevens, tom perkins, jim bassett, alyssa holmquist, devin mcconkey, sergio ortiz, otoniel solis, jack nyman, john lessl <u>hks</u> jess corrigan, aia, principal in charge tom holt, project manager gerald ward, project architect johnny luttrul, construction admin. manager robert taylor jou jou wang
color + design consultant_	april greiman
landscape architect_	caye cook & associate
structural + civil engineer_	walter p. moore + associates, inc.
m/e/p engineer_	bartlett cocke, lp

Buildings do not instruct, they only accommodate and, hopefully, inspire. Such was the common wisdom up until the mid-seventies when Michel Foucault re-introduced us to the Panopticon and suggested that "disciplinary" institutions constructed our social existence, if not our very selves. The prison, the factory, the hospital, and the school all functioned as social "technologies" in which instruction or training was implicitly encoded in a sequence of spaces tied to a program of normative behavior. Foucault's disturbing idea that institutions form us, rather than we them, was outrageous in its time. It effectively turned our ideas regarding "functionalism" inside out. No longer mere accommodation or use, function came to stand for something that was wholly contrived, if not outright manipulative (and something that was politically and economically motivated). Foucault's description constituted an inversion of our understanding of functional accommodation, an inversion that we are still grappling with today.

We have largely grappled with this redefinition of functionalism by assuring ourselves that Foucault was a historian researching conditions that existed at the turn of the nineteenth century, on the other side of the modernist divide. Modern architecture dispensed with the overt social agendas that were built into traditional architecture—such as the monumental expression of authority—and attempted to reestablish architecture as functional accommodation driven by its own autonomous logic. As a result, we have been able to conveniently neglect Foucault's disturbing analysis. Modern buildings are imagined to be ideologically transparent containers, more or less functional, more or less beautiful, and more or less grounded in the art of the discipline. Modern buildings influence and inspire and they do function, but they do not instruct. They are not the purview of politicians, or behavioralists or social engineers but of the creative imagination. The idea that a Modern architecture could manipulate the behavior of its inhabitants or otherwise "construct" its subjects calls into question its very existence.

I would like to draw attention to a flagrant contradiction in what one might call the naive functionalism of Modern architecture: the School of Architecture. In the School of Architecture, the idea that buildings themselves "instruct" is unabashedly pursued; training is the order of the day and the idea of (re)constructing the identity of the student/architect forms its overt logic. As opposed to a lecture, a book, or a practice session, the idea that an institutional building would serve to indoctrinate a student is often accepted without question. Spatializing an overt program— the distribution of students, for example, in a series of partitioned workstations—is intended to construct new subjects as only buildings can. We routinely call this built-in, disciplinary logic "studio culture." It remains in effect (as those of us who teach would have it) 24 hours a day, seven days a week.

This training function is on the agenda of some of the most important buildings of the twentieth century, including the Bauhaus, Taliesin West, Crown Hall, and Carpenter Center. These acknowledged "masterpieces" function in a unique dual role, as both canonical works of architecture in themselves and, at the same time, the institutional means by which the canon is imparted to future generations. In other words, these buildings function on two somewhat incompatible levels; they are both the content and the vehicle for the delivery of that content. They are not only the books in the library but the library itself, they are not only the paintings in a museum collection but the institution that exhibits art, they compose not only the musical score but the concert hall in which the score is received. As canonical works they are meant to inspire, enhance and influence; but as institutional buildings—schools—they are also meant to indoctrinate vis-à-vis studio culture. Because of this dual role, architecture schools can be said to form one of the most significant subsets of the modern canon. The Architecture School is, in effect, the institution that produces other institutions; it is a school of schools.

While it is clear that the propagation of a canon and the propagation of disciplinary training constitute two different forms of social interaction, it is unclear as to whether these two functions could ever be reconciled to each other. Most schools manage to train, fewer manage to inspire, and those that inspire often do so by suppressing the training function. While you can certainly study architecture in a cathedral—Crown Hall has proven this—you can also study architecture in a spec office building filled with partitioned workstations. The point is that neither solution is adequate in addressing the problem that the School of Architecture poses and the potential that this school among schools actually possesses. This potential can be described as that specific interaction of building and program wherein that which inspires—the canon—comes to sublimate the idea of programmatic "training" that Foucault introduced so many years ago.

This brief analysis of the School of Architecture will serve as both the introduction and the critical lens though which I will look at a recent addition to this most significant subset of the Modern canon: Roto Architects School of Architecture at the University of Texas at Prairie View. I believe the building directly addresses the problem posed by the School of Architecture. It speaks of an informed functionalism that goes beyond the limitations implied by the school-as-cathedral and the school-as-spec office block.

Four Stages

Earlier I defined a Modern building as transparent accommodation driven by an autonomous logic. I hope it is clear that the accommodation or function of a building is often far from transparent; that it possesses institutional agendas that go beyond the workings of a naive functionalism. Too often it is the institutional agenda alone that constitutes a school. An obvious example of this would be an elementary "school" consisting of trailers set out on an asphalt parking lot. In a School of Architecture, the institutional agenda might consist only of partitioned workstations spread across standardized floor-plates. What Modern architecture added to the institutional function, of course, is the autonomous logic that is inherent to its practice. This logic constitutes the substance of the canon and, conversely, the canon subsequently constitutes the autonomous logic. What this means, simply, is that the rules/logic by which we develop a project are partially encoded in the canonical works of the discipline itself. This rigorous, inbuilt logic is characteristic of Roto's architecture in general, and of their Prairie View school in particular. I would now like to explore how Roto used these rules to sublimate the institutional imperative inherent in the program type and to resolve the contradiction between the reproduction of the canon and the training function inherent in the program type.

The intrinsic logic of our architecture is best revealed by hypothetically reconstructing the development of the building's design. The clarity of the logic, as well as its didactic character make this a relatively easy task. This reconstruction will be divided into four discrete stages. Imagine the starting point of our school as a simple H-shaped block turned on its side. This serves as a distillation of the massing as two parallel concrete framed blocks with bridges crossing over a void between them. From this starting point one simple operation sets the developmental logic of the building into motion. This operation consists of the orthogonal shifting of the south block one bay to the east. This shift does several things at once. It responds to the entrance of the Prairie View campus and the building's important corner situation. The shift also sets up the logic of a front or "head," building at this strategic location. The shift also sets up a spatial condition at the two ends of the buildings creating a formal courtyard at one end of the building and a service plaza at the other. The shift also has a significant effect on the interior. It creates a sheared space between the blocks prompting the complex play of stairs, bridges, and ramps. We refer to this interior volume as an "exchange space," and it figures prominently in the programmatic operation of the building.

Following the slippage of the two blocks, the second stage of development concerns the relation between the concrete frame structure of the primary massing and their associated brick skins. (The craft of these skins are amazing, the subtly corbelled construction results in an animated surface module that is almost alive in its effect.) As in the center space of the building, the initial shifting of the blocks seems to activate the building skins setting up a complex frame/skin relation unique to each block. On the northern block, the skin lies loosely around the volume; its wobbly geometry gives it the appearance of a billowing fabric tacked down to the frame at strategic points. This brick fabric covers the entire volume creating a lateral façade facing north toward the bulk of the campus. On the south block, the relation of the fabric to the skin is entirely different. Here, the shifting of the block to the west seems to have torn the skin from the block completely. The displaced skin is thus free to form the complex sheathing of the head building leaving the concrete frame of the south block almost entirely exposed to the elements.

It is the formation of the head building or auditorium that constitutes the third stage of the building's diagrammatic logic and what is perhaps the most significant design feature of the project. In their descriptions, we refer to this appendage

as the origin of the primary ordering lines. This does not mean, however that the auditorium is constituted as the dominant element within the project. I put "head" building in quotation marks because it is ambiguous whether the auditorium is the primary focal point of the building or merely a secondary appendage shot out from the south block. This ambiguity operates to the benefit of the building; it solves a major programmatic contradiction. The appendage contains a separate institution called the Cultural Center for African American History in Texas. Located in the "head" building it must exist both as a separate entity and as part of the larger complex that includes the School of Architecture. This equivocal status of the appendage is important because, despite the significance of the Cultural Center, it is not the programmatic driver of the building. Seen in this way, the logic behind the auditorium's ambiguous connection to the main mass becomes clear. It is shifted off the central axis and only tentatively attached to the south bar by the brick skin as described above. This plastic tour-de-force precisely mirrors the complexity of the relationship of the two programmatic entities.

Finally, the fourth and last stage of design development concerns the metal cladding of the building that occurs on the south elevation as well as on the eastern wall of the treed courtyard. Though made of metal columns covered by a perforated mesh skin, these screens are not an extension of the frame and skin logic already discussed for the rest of the building. As the brick skin slipped off of the southern block to form the appendage or head building, it exposed the elevation of the block to harsh environmental conditions. The response to this condition appears at first glance to be of an ad-hoc or provisional construction. I call it provisional because the material and geometry of the steel framed cladding is altogether alien to the rest of the structure. This difference is highly exaggerated. The frames appear propped into place against the side of the southern block. It is also important to note that they are made out of standardized steel tubes and corrugated metal sheets that contrast the customized fabric of the rest of the building—the brickwork for example, and the idiosyncratic shapes of the appendage. This pragmatic solution to the problem created by the exposed elevation shows an entirely different sensibility at play in the building.

The autonomous logic of the two slipped blocks and the subsequent deployment of bridges, ramps, skins, appendages, and cladding, constitute the formal devices that animate the building but do not encompass its logic. If this were the case, we would be examining an exercise in formalism, and formalism always comes at the cost of a naive understanding of function. It is in the handling of the deeper implications of the training function that Roto's building makes a significant contribution to the School of Architecture.

Exchange Space

The autonomous logic of the building constitutes the formal devices through which the training function is constructed. They are also the devices through which that function is ultimately sublimated. How do you both construct the institution and overcome it at the same time? Not by resorting to irony, built-in contradiction or any other forms of logical confusion built into the form of the building. The answer lies in the creation of subjectivities, specifically the creation of subjectivities that exceed those produced by training. I will explain what this means.

In spite of our naïve understanding of Modern functionalism, buildings construct us as subjects. To repeat, buildings produce us as much as we produce them. This is done by encoding institutional programs into forms—forms that are calculated to produce a certain range of practical behavior. This understanding of subjectivity led Foucault to an appreciation of the built environment as a distributed network of power relations capable of creating, in its entirety, an extended social field. While this may summarize Foucault's analysis with regards to the built environment, it should not limit the implications of his analysis. While the buildings we make do produce subjectivities, it is important to remember that they are not necessarily the docile and defeated subjectivities produced by the disciplinary logic of the prisons, the factories, the hospitals, and the schools discussed by Foucault. In this regard, the projection of alternate subjectivities becomes our principal concern. This concern cannot be addressed until we are willing to concede the powers at play upon us. And while it is true there is hardly anyone outside of the discipline who is prepared to grant such importance to the built environment, the designers of this environment must nevertheless be willing to take responsibility for it. They must, in other words, be willing to address the problem of subjectivity. Roto's school does this. It creates an alternative to the subject called "architect" in a remarkable way.

The construction of an alternate subjectivity would seem a huge task were it not for the fact that we do it every time we design a building. That we often do this unawares does not change the fact. The problem is how to set about creating subjectivity in a more determined fashion. This is where Rot̲o's building becomes instructive. To begin, we might ask: what elements of the building contribute to the construction of a subjectivity that exceeds that which is produced by mere training? Here we can return to effects produced by the school's formal devices. Examining the building from a broader social perspective, we can see that its programmatic logic is organized around two significant axes. These two axes produce circuits of interaction within the sructure around which specific subjectivities are formed. The first axis is the vertical axis that establishes an above/below organization of the building, and the second is the horizontal (longitudinal) axis that establishes its back/front organization. I would like to look at the programmatic development of both of these axes in turn.

The institutional program of the School of Architecture develops floor-to-floor around the vertical axis of the building moving from bottom to top, one program built upon the next. On the ground floor, public entry spaces, administrative offices, lecture hall, fabrication shop and formal galleries, give way to a second floor of classrooms, faculty offices, library, and a digital lab. This stratification forms an integrated vertical machine devoted to the various stages of architectural training. This stratification has as its destination the largest spaces in the building, the studio/loft spaces that occupy the entire third floor floorplate. These spaces are ultimately bound for subdivision into cubicle cells or workstations, one cubicle per student. With the studio loft space as its destination, the section transforms programmatically as it moves upwards from the associated collective spaces at the base of the building to the individual cubicles at the top. This upward movement can be seen to finally focus architectural

training directly upon the individual activities of the student. While the size of the lofts gives the studio function its importance, their subdivision gives it an individualized or personal significance. In this manner, the program built up along the vertical axis constructs an individual subject in a progression toward the cellular subdivision of the studio. As a consolidated block, housed in the top-most reach of the building, these cellular spaces constitute an incubator of the famous architectural ego.

The horizontal axis functions in a similar, cumulative way by transforming a sequence of programmatic layers into a machine-like apparatus. Cutting across the grain of the vertical movement, the horizontal axis structures a program that pulls together diffuse and various activities into a promenade that moves from the back service end of the Architecture School to the front ceremonial end of the Cultural Center. This promenade is drawn toward the theatre or head building that serves as a focus for the organization of the ground plan. At a pragmatic level, the axis connects the public elements of the Architecture School and mixes them in with the Cultural Center creating a sequence that unifies these two incongruent entities. The sequence of lecture halls, two galleries, archive, offices, ceremonial courtyard, and finally the theater, create out of the two programmatic entities a third. Yet this is secondary to the main objective that is to shape for the occupants of both institutions a collective identity. As opposed to the individually focused subject construction developed along the vertical axis of architectural training, the horizontal axis produces its adversary and complement, a collective subject.

The movement along the two axes, from bottom to top and from back to front (from private to public, individual to collective) suggests an older mode of subjectivisation, the architectural promenade. The architectural promenade was invented by Corbusier as a didactic mechanism to instruct the inhabitant about the world around her, whether that world be a historical worldview (Mundaneum) or an idealized landscape (Villa Savoye). In Roto's building, however, I employed the linear schema for descriptive purposes only. The building does not operate along one sequential path, or even two. Instead of a promenade, circuits of interaction structured by horizontal and vertical axes are a function of the bridges, ramps and stairs occupying the sheared space between the primary blocks. More than a scripted promenade moving from bottom to top, these circuits form discrete patterns of movement that are sequential and cumulative but also eccentric, random and intermittent. They are given added force by being not only ceremonial, but habitual, repetitive, and routinized. The programmatic components of the building are inscribed and reinscribed by the patterns of movement through the building's so-called "exchange space." I would argue that these habitual patterns produce a kind of subjectivity in which we can recognize the education of an architect.

Conclusion

To briefly recap the argument, two axes form the social organization of the school. These axes generate circuits of movement that produce individuation in the loft, and collectivisation in the theatre. It is the organization of these subjectivities by the autonomous logic of the building that allows them to transcend the subjectivities produced by institutional programming or mere training. What is the difference between subjectivities produced by Roto's building on the Prairie View campus and those produced by a spec office building filled with workstations? The answer can come in the form of another question: what is the difference between an architect and a CAD operator or, alternately, what is the difference between a sensibility and a ten-step program? In other words, the answer is that difference.

It would seem that there is much we can learn from a School of Architecture—the school of all schools—not the least of which would be the limitations of our routine practices. The assumption of a transparent or naive functionality has obscured the survival of disciplinary programs well into the modern period. It has also blocked a clear understanding of the potential that exists in the production of subjectivity. Soon, there may be no other logic with which to defend the School of Architecture, or any other school, against a functional deployment of standardized spaces. Everything will become the equivalent of trailers in the parking lot. At that time, the need to construct that subjectivity called "architect" will have to be understood clearly if it is to survive. Crown Hall and all the other cathedrals of learning will be of no help. Architecture that addresses the problem of subjectivity, like Roto's school, will hold the key.

234
+

2005   100,000 Stupas, Land of Medicine Buddha   *Santa Cruz, CA*

Architecture and Art Building, Prairie View A&M University   *Prairie View, TX*

Boys and Girls Club of Hollywood   *Hollywood, CA*

Council District 7, Neighborhood City Hall   *Los Angeles, CA*

Hamlet Restaurants   *West Hollywood, CA*

Hollywood Orange Building   *Hollywood, CA*

Fallen Firefighters Memorial, Los Angeles Fire Department   *Los Angeles, CA*

Philo House   *Mendocino County, CA*

Silver Lake Hotel   *Los Angeles, CA*

Sunset Boulevard Center   *Los Angeles, CA*

Vogt Commons   *Louisville, KY*

2004   Ari Bhod Retreat   *Tehachapi, CA*

ASU West Gateway Vision Plan   *Tempe, AZ*

Cliffside House   *Malibu, CA*

From The Verandah, UCLA Fowler Museum   *Los Angeles, CA*

Kohala Center   *Kohala, HI*

UCSD La Jolla Play Development and Education Center   *La Jolla, CA*

2003   Center for Art and Culture Competition   *Hefei, China*

Still Points Exhibition, Southern California Institute of Architecture   *Los Angeles, CA*

Gompertz House   *Livingston, MT*

West Hollywood Housing   *West Hollywood, CA*

2002   Adventure Retreat   *Santa Monica Mountains, CA*

Corner Table Ranch   *Billings, MT*

iBlast offices   *Los Angeles, CA*

Joshua Tree House   *Joshua Tree, CA*

Los Gatos House   *Los Gatos, CA*

Lux Pictures Offices   *Los Angeles, CA*

Monte Argentario Agri-Resort Competition   *Monte Argentario, Italy*

Red Canyon Ranch Restoration   *Sheridan, MT*

2001 Amalfi Resort *Amalfi Coast, Italy*

Forest Refuge Buddhist Retreat *Barre, MA*

Oak Pass House *Beverly Hills, CA*

Ontario Educational Village Design Competition *Ontario, CA*

Liberty Wildlife Rehabilitation Center *Scottsdale, AZ*

Museo de las Americas *Denver, CO*

Sacred Springs Native Culture Center, University High School *Los Angeles, CA*

2000 Deere House *Bel Air, CA*

Miller-Schaaf Masterplan *Bozeman, MT*

Vail House *Vail, CO*

1999 House in Sagaponac *Long Island, NY*

Steven Walker Residence *Hollywood Hills, CA*

1998 Miracle Manor Retreat *Desert Hot Springs, CA*

Sinte Gleska University *Rosebud, SD*
Master Plan Student Center, Technology Building, Multipurpose Building

Soledad Enrichment Action's Camp Unity *Angeles Crest National Forest, CA*

1997 Xiyuan Buddhist Monastery School *Suzhou, China*

Performing Arts and Teaching Center, Oglala Lakota College *Kyle, SD*

Reebok Inner City Stores

Warehouse C *Nagasaki, Japan*

1996 Carlson Reges House *Los Angeles, CA*

New Jersey Residence *Bernardsville, NJ*

1995 Gemini Consulting's Learning Center *Morristown, NJ*

1994 Dorland Mountain Arts Colony *Temecula, CA*

"Urban Revisions, Current Projects for the Public Realm," Museum of Contemporary Art *Los Angeles, CA*

1993 CDLT 1,2 *Los Angeles, CA*

Nicola Restaurant *Los Angeles, CA*

Santa Monica College Library Competition *Los Angeles, CA*

1992 RedRoTo, Creation Square *Yokohama, Japan*

Southern California Institute of Architecture *Los Angeles, CA*

1991 Circolo Restaurant *Glendale, CA*

credits

photograph

photographers	firm	page numbers
Adam Gerndt	RoTo Architects, Inc.	177-179
April Greiman	Made in Space, Inc.	166-171
Assassi Productions		27, 30-40, 56, 73, 75, 78-83, 85, 180-185, 212-214, 216-217, 220-225, 227
Benny Chan	Fotoworks	17, 19-21, 23, 128-129, 132-137
David Guthrie		215, 218-219
Forest Fulton	RoTo Architects, Inc.	176, 178-179
James Bassett	RoTo Architects, Inc.	140-141, 148-149, 186-193
Jeff Goldberg	ESTO	46-49, 52-55, 57-63, 66-69
John Lodge	Lodge Studio	163, 166, 172-173, 204
Katsuhisa Kida		92
Kim Swarts		22
Kiyokazu Arai		93, 100-101
Lorna Turner		70-71,74,76
RMA Photography, Inc.		200-202, 204-205
RoTo Architects, Inc.		16, 18-19, 28-30, 33, 35, 41, 52, 73, 78, 90, 93, 98, 106-107, 114, 118-119, 126-128, 162-167, 172, 174-175, 178-179, 182, 185, 203, 206-207, 213
Shinkenchiku-Sha		96-99,101,104-105
SS Kyusyu Co., Ltd.		88-89,91-92,94-95,101-103

design

design / production

April Greiman	Made in Space, Inc., Los Angeles	
Lucile Cook		
Arisa Chen		
Marci Boudreau	Picnic Design, Los Angeles	

production / coordination

Janine Coughlin
Alex Pettas
Pamela Romero

edit

editors

Aino Paasonen
Linda Hart
Aram Saroyan

Walking side-by-side with a similar cadence, ebbing and flowing, we moved through the moss garden of Saijo-Ji, also known as Kokedera, looking and gesturing without hands or with a nod of our heads, almost speaking. It was as if we were echoing what we were seeing and each other's perceptions. My body was one sense feeling and knowing everything at once. This was the first time I remember this happening, although it seemed completely familiar. Periodically we uttered a few words to each other, "The same for me," was the response, expressed in a gesture.

Over forty varieties of moss blend into a single, fine, luxuriant texture carpeting the entire garden. This is a place for contemplation. When we arrived late morning the light was strong enough to intensify the colors of the moss and maples but by late afternoon the mood of this remarkable place changed to dark and primeval. At the base of a conifer, a thin membrane of moss covered the root system of the tree but barely the earth. The moss continued up a small embankment covering the entire slope of the hillside. A stream of water rupturing the membrane revealed the substrate, getting deeper as it reached the bottom.

A cross-section revealed the layers of organic matter. Each layer revealed some aspect of the next, or was it the next also. One layer existed with the other; each was the other. What normally helped me distinguish one thing from another existed only in my thoughts. Distinct boundaries were non-existent—it was all one thing; unity and diversity. This was another place to pause and stare for a while.

There we were, released from anticipation or recollection, seeing with greater and greater focus, the detail that was not present a moment before, as if we were able to see what was barely visible.

The trajectory of the line of the stream continuing down the hill carried it over a small embankment and onto the narrow top edge of a big rock splitting the water into two halves, which fell in sheets into a large, shimmering pond, creating an elliptical pattern. I had never seen water shape shift like that. I felt like I was seeing the world for the first time as a child. So much was happening all around us.

I wondered how it evolved into this state. Was this natural? Had it always been this way, or was this the invisible hand of the gardener we were witnessing? Maybe it was both; in subtle and nurturing ways, he enhanced what was latent. We walked until we arrived at the verandah of the temple. It was long, open to an enclosed, rectangular garden, the same size and proportion of the inner room of the shrine. We sat at what felt like the centerline of both, and the edge of each.

In between, in the garden there were three objects in the space: two specimen trees flanked a stone lantern. In the room there were also three objects; a mirroring of the outside. The temperature was dropping as the sun was setting. We began to drink our warm, thick green tea, held in special cups and sipped in slow motion. The coolness of the air was more evident as the warm liquid went down.

> *At that moment, the sky was turning orange.*
> *cool air*
> *warm tea*
> *orange sky*
> *symmetrical space*
> *both of us sitting at the midpoint*
> *sensing the still point*
> *almost weightless*

I felt compelled to describe this intensely sensuous moment and as I began to speak we looked at each other and realized the experience was our common ground. No words were needed. We smiled and she said,

"In the tea ceremony this is what is referred to as speaking in silence."